THE GOOD LANDLORD HANDBOOK

THE GOOD LANDLORD HANDBOOK

SUCCEED AS A LANDLORD UNDER THE RENTERS' RIGHTS ACT

SUZANNE SMITH

C

CENTURY

CENTURY

UK | USA | Canada | Ireland | Australia
India | New Zealand | South Africa

Century is part of the Penguin Random House group of companies
whose addresses can be found at global.penguinrandomhouse.com

Penguin Random House UK,
One Embassy Gardens, 8 Viaduct Gardens, London SW11 7BW

penguin.co.uk

Penguin Random House UK

First published 2026
001

Cover design: Marc Riley
Photo credit (front cover): Suzanne Smith Photo credit (back cover):
Louise Haywood-Schiefer

Printed and bound in Great Britain by Clays Ltd, Elcograf S.p.A.

The authorised representative in the EEA is Penguin Random House Ireland,
Morrison Chambers, 32 Nassau Street, Dublin D02 YH68

A CIP catalogue record for this book is available from the British Library

ISBN: 978–1–807–84396–0

Penguin Random House is committed to a sustainable future for our business, our readers and our planet. This book is made from Forest Stewardship Council® certified paper.

MIX
Paper
FSC® C018179

To my lovely husband, whose idea it was for me to write this book.

And to my dear friend Patricia Ogunfeibo who gave me so much valuable feedback while I was writing it.

CONTENTS

PART II

BEFORE THE TENANCY

PART III
DURING THE TENANCY

PART IV
ENDING THE TENANCY

INTRODUCTION

The Renters' Rights Act 2025 is the biggest shake-up to England's private rented sector in almost 40 years. Complex rules are now in force at every stage of a tenancy, and if we are to succeed as landlords, we need to be professional, organised and focused on providing a high-quality service for tenants in compliance with the new rules.

That's where *The Good Landlord Handbook* comes in.

1. How this book will help you

Landlord compliance is often shrouded in mystery, with service providers claiming the rules are too difficult for the average landlord to understand, let alone cope with the Renters' Rights Act (RRA). I disagree.

The RRA has overhauled how we landlords need to run our businesses, and we need to do things differently. This book seeks to demystify these changes and equip you with the knowledge you need to operate within the new framework.

There is a stand-alone part on the RRA in the book to make it easy for you to understand what has changed. I have also integrated the new rules into every chapter, as this is now the way we need to operate.

Whether you're an experienced landlord, just starting out or someone wanting to "raise their game", this practical handbook takes you through each stage of a tenancy and shows you how to succeed as a good landlord with happy tenants. It combines clear, actionable guidance on compliance with practical advice on dealing with tricky issues.

The ethos of the "good landlord" underpins everything in this book. Good landlords have happier tenants who stay longer and look after the property better. Being a good landlord is a win-win, as it makes good business sense and provides a positive experience for tenants.

This book assumes you already own a rental property and helps you with the challenges of being a landlord, from finding great tenants to managing your properties and keeping your costs down whilst providing an excellent service to your tenants.

It includes specific advice for landlords of properties who let to single households (called single lets), or to sharers (called Houses in Multiple Occupation or HMOs), where appropriate. It doesn't cover buying rental properties or investment strategies, as those subjects merit a book in their own right!

If you're not a landlord, but you provide products or services to landlords, this book will give you an invaluable insight into best practice for landlords.

In writing this book, I draw on experience as a self-managing landlord of a portfolio of Victorian buy-to-let properties, together with my 25 years as a solicitor working in business. It also includes answers to the many questions I've received about what it takes to be a successful landlord and navigate the changes that the RRA brings to landlords in the private rented sector.

Finally, the Renters' Rights Act is complex new legislation which is open to different interpretations. I've set out my understanding of the law in this book to the best of my ability, but I might not be right, or entirely right. My guidance is general and cannot account for the particular facts of your situation. This book is not a substitute for legal advice, and you should consult a specialist housing solicitor for advice on your own circumstances.

2. The changing private rented sector

The implementation of the tenancy reforms in the Renters' Rights Act on 1 May 2026 came during a period of enormous change for landlords, coinciding with the start of the roll-out of Making Tax Digital.[1] Significant changes to the minimum energy efficiency standards for rental properties are also due in 2030.

The RRA represents a significant shift for the English private rented sector. On the day of Royal Assent, Minister for Housing and Planning, Matthew Pennycook, said the Act would "level decisively the playing field between landlord and tenant and transform the experience of private renting".[2]

The last major change in the PRS was when Margaret Thatcher's government deregulated the private rented sector

---

1. See HM Revenue & Customs, *Making Tax Digital for Income Tax*, https://www.gov.uk/government/collections/making-tax-digital-for-income-tax.
2. Ministry of Housing, Communities and Local Government, *Historic Renters' Rights Act Becomes Law*, 27 October 2025, https://www.gov.uk/government/news/historic-renters-rights-act-becomes-law.

with the Housing Act 1988 and the Housing Act 1996. Those Housing Acts tipped the playing field in favour of landlords, making it easier for landlords to regain possession of their properties and increase rents.

However, the RRA has reversed some of those changes and restricts the freedoms for landlords in those Housing Acts. It has fundamentally changed how landlords have been operating since assured shorthold tenancies became the default tenancy in 1997.

3. Key changes in the Renters' Rights Act

The RRA amended the Housing Act 1988 (HA88) to create a periodic assured tenancy in a new section 4A HA88. This became the default tenancy in England on 1 May 2026. (To avoid confusion, in this book I refer to this new assured tenancy as an assured periodic tenancy or APT).

Subject to certain transitional arrangements for on-going possession proceedings,[3] all existing assured shorthold tenancies (ASTs) were converted into assured periodic tenancies on 1 May 2026, and no new ASTs can be granted to tenants.

The new default tenancy is now periodic, without a fixed-term period or an end date. Under the old system, an AST was typically granted for an initial fixed-term period of 6 to 12 months, during which neither party could terminate it, unless there was a break clause allowing a party to terminate it early.

This means there is now no minimum length of a tenancy. Furthermore, a tenant may serve two months' notice to quit at

3. See Appendix 4: Implementation.

any time. Previously, unless there was a break clause in the tenancy agreement, tenants could only leave after the fixed term had ended.

It is a big change, as landlords no longer have the comfort of knowing their tenants will stay for the length of the initial fixed term. Planning is harder for properties with a higher natural turnover of tenants, such as flats and HMOs. It is also now very challenging for landlords who specialise in letting to students, as they can no longer have a fixed term that mirrors the academic year.

RRA also abolished "no fault" evictions, which enabled landlords to evict a tenant without having to state a reason. Landlords can now only bring a tenancy to an end if they have a valid ground under section 8 of the Housing Act 1988 (HA88).

The tenancy reforms brought in many other new rules for landlords, which I explain in Chapter 2.

4. What is a good landlord?

Although I understandably talk a lot about the RRA in this book, it's important to keep in mind the "why" and the "how" of being a landlord. After all, Parliament has introduced various laws to set minimum standards for landlords to ensure we provide decent homes for tenants to live in. As Maslow's hierarchy of needs shows us, physiological needs such as secure housing are essential for human wellbeing.[4]

When the RRA was going through Parliament, there was much

4. Maslow, A. H. (1943), "A theory of human motivation", *Psychological Review*, 50(4), 370–396, https://psychclassics.yorku.ca/Maslow/motivation.htm.

reference to the terms "good landlords" and "responsible landlords".

In the second reading debate on the Renters' Rights Bill in the House of Commons, the then Deputy Prime Minister, Angela Rayner, said they valued the "contribution made by responsible landlords who provide quality homes to their tenants". Minister for Housing and Planning, Matthew Pennycook, said that "good landlords have nothing to fear" from the reforms.[5]

When the Mayor of Greater Manchester, Andy Burnham, announced the creation of the Greater Manchester Good Landlord Charter in 2023,[6] he described good landlords as those "trying to do the right thing".

The terms "good landlord" and "responsible landlord" aren't legal terms and they're not included in the RRA. This is because, from a legal perspective, landlords either comply with the law or they don't. There's no concept in law of a landlord being "responsible" or "good" that goes beyond compliance with their many legal responsibilities.

However, I believe that being a "good landlord" is a useful concept for landlords. It recognises that housing is different from other products and services. Good landlords have a sense of social responsibility and balance the needs of their tenants

5. House of Commons, 'Renters' Rights Bill', *Hansard*, 9 October 2024, vol. 754, col. 332, https://hansard.parliament.uk/commons/2024-10-09/debates/7A308DDD-EC0A-4F2D-9C18-664E12D5BC92/Renters%E2%80%99Rights Bill.
6. "Housing 2023: Andy Burnham's keynote speech in full", *Housing Digital* (27 June 2023), https://housingdigital.co.uk/housing-2023-andy-burnhams-keynote-speech-in-full.

with the fact that being a private landlord is a business and not the provision of social housing.

The entry-level requirement for being a good landlord goes beyond mere compliance with the letter of the law. It means complying with the spirit and intent of the law, not trying to wriggle out of things or find technical loopholes. The law is the minimum standard, and good landlords shouldn't stop there. Instead, they try to do the right thing, even if it means doing more than is strictly necessary under the law.

5. Don't landlords earn "passive" income?

In a word, no.

Framing the role of a landlord as "passive" is the wrong mindset and is factually inaccurate. It implies that it's possible to make money as a landlord with little time, effort or responsibility. Like getting interest in a bank account or receiving dividends from shares. Just a quick check-in from time to time.

Being a successful landlord requires a lot of upfront effort and expertise, which includes sourcing, financing and refurbishing new properties and finding good tenants. Sure, it's possible to outsource these activities, but the more landlords outsource, the lower the profit. Finding trustworthy people to outsource to can be a challenge, especially for newbies. Even finding good letting agents is very hit and miss.

Once you've got your tenants in place, it doesn't stop there. The properties and the tenants need managing. You can delegate the tasks to your letting agent's property management department, but it may cost you around 15% of the gross rent. They may also add a mark-up on repairs and maintenance work. Some agents charge extras such as "compliance fees".

Whilst it's certainly possible for landlords to take a more passive role by outsourcing, they still carry the can. They should oversee their agents and be sufficiently knowledgeable to ensure their property and tenants are properly looked after. If a serious problem arises, it is for the landlord to assess the situation and decide how to resolve it.

Outsourcing also reduces a landlord's profit, when margins may already be tight.

Even if landlords find excellent agents, they should still visit their properties at least once a year. I've heard too many first-hand accounts from landlords who trusted their agents, only to find their properties or tenants were neglected.

Landlords have a lot of legal duties, especially following the implementation of the reforms in the Renters' Rights Act. The term "passive" income downplays the risks and responsibilities that come with being a landlord. Landlords provide homes for people to live in, and that can't ever be passive.

The best way to make sure it's being done properly is to make sure you understand the rules. You're in the right place for this. The purpose of *The Good Landlord Handbook* is to help landlords understand how to be successful as a good landlord, whether they choose to use agents or handle it themselves.

6. The design of this handbook

The handbook is divided into four distinct parts.

Part I lays the foundations for landlords, explaining the business aspects, before giving an overview of the Renters' Rights Act 2025, the key legal obligations of landlords and how to choose and use letting agents.

The remaining three parts mirror the journey you will take with each tenancy.

Part II explains the actions landlords need to take before the tenancy to ensure the property is ready. This involves setting the rent, finding tenants, tenant selection and referencing and setting up a new tenancy.

The handbook then moves on to Part III, which goes through what you need to know during the tenancy, once your tenants have moved in, including property management, HMOs, inspections, the new rules regarding rent increases, managing rent arrears and common problems that arise during a tenancy.

Part IV covers the end of the tenancy.

Where relevant, I explain how the rules differ for tenancies where the rent is more than £100,000 a year. They are known as "high rent" or "non-Housing Act" tenancies, as they are outside the ambit of the Housing Act 1988.

You will find references to useful information in the Appendices at the end, including a section on further support, links to the various statutes and regulations in Appendix 2: Legislation and a full Bibliography.

Finally, I send a free weekly newsletter that cuts through the noise so you know what's happening and what to do about it. You can sign up at **theindependentlandlord.com/subscribe**.

Let's start by looking at the business of being a landlord, the first chapter of Part I: Foundations.

PART I

FOUNDATIONS

CHAPTER 1

THE BUSINESS OF BEING A LANDLORD

This chapter introduces the core concepts of the business of being a private landlord in England, including the key strategies and how landlords make money.

It will help you make your rental business profitable, while maintaining high standards for your tenants and focusing on the needs of your tenants when making decisions.

In short, it explains how being a good landlord is good business.

1. What is a private landlord?

There are approximately 2.4 million private landlords in England, providing homes for 11 million tenants.[1] Yet the word landlord carries negative connotations, and people often pair it with adjectives like "rogue", "unscrupulous" or even "criminal".

However, I haven't come across a suitable alternative to landlord. Some people use "property investor", but to me,

1. Ministry of Housing, Communities and Local Government, *English Private Landlord Survey 2024: Main Report,* https://www.gov.uk/government/statistics/english-private-landlord-survey-2024-main-report/english-private-landlord-profi-2024-main-report.

that's more appropriate for flipping, i.e., buying a property and reselling it at a profit after a short period.

So, what is a private landlord?

A landlord is someone who owns a property and rents it to someone else in return for rent. In other words, a housing provider. Landlords are sub-divided into two further categories: private landlords and social landlords.

Social landlords are registered with the Regulator of Social Housing and provide low cost rental accommodation, or social housing, to tenants.[2] Examples include local authorities and housing associations.

Private landlords, by contrast, are individuals or companies who rent out properties to tenants and are able to charge a market rent. According to the *2024 English Private Landlord Survey*,[3] the overwhelming majority of private landlords (83%) own one to four properties, me included, and these represent 51% of tenancies. 17% of landlords own five or more properties, or 49% of tenancies.

In this book, when I refer to a landlord, I mean a "private landlord", unless I specifically refer to social landlords.

Buy-to-let landlords

A buy-to-let landlord is a private landlord who buys a residential property specifically to rent to tenants. Usually, they buy the property with a specialist buy-to-let mortgage

2. Regulator of Social Housing, *Register, De-register or Make a Notification*, https://www.gov.uk/guidance/registrations-de-registrations-and-notifications.
3. Ibid.

designed specifically for landlords. That said, according to the *2024 English Private Landlord Survey,* 41% of landlords reported having no borrowing for their rental properties, with 42% having an interest-only buy-to-let mortgage and 15% a repayment buy-to-let mortgage.

Buy-to-let landlords are a relatively recent phenomenon. They emerged as a significant force in the housing market following legislative changes after the Housing Act 1988 introduced assured shorthold tenancies (ASTs), which allowed landlords to charge market rents and regain possession of their properties more easily through "no fault evictions" under section 21.

The introduction of ASTs as the default tenancy under the Housing Act 1996 reduced the risks for landlords in letting properties and provided landlords with greater confidence. Coupled with the introduction in 1996 of buy-to-let mortgages, property became a mainstream investment and significantly grew the sector.

However, the RRA abolished ASTs on 1 May 2026, and assured periodic tenancies (APTs) became the default.

Accidental landlords

Whereas many landlords deliberately enter the rental market by purchasing a buy-to-let, others become landlords unintentionally.

These "accidental landlords" might inherit a property, relocate for work while keeping their original home, or move in with a partner who already owns a property. Rather than selling, they decide to let the property out.

Landlords who started "accidentally", so to speak, make up a significant proportion of landlords. According to the *2024 English Private Landlord Survey*, 37% of landlords started out as accidental landlords.

It is important to remember that the law treats accidental landlords the same as professional investors and there are no exemptions for accidental landlords.

If they have a mortgage, they must contact their lender, as usually residential mortgages don't allow lettings. Although many lenders give consent to let the property, they may require you to switch to a buy-to-let mortgage, subject to any stress tests.

A stress test is a check that lenders use to assess whether landlords can afford their buy-to-let mortgage repayments if interest rates increase. It involves assessing whether the rental income will cover the mortgage payments, typically requiring it to exceed the payments by a set percentage (e.g. 125–145%).

2. Why landlords need to be tenant-centric

Just as successful consumer goods companies focus on customer satisfaction, successful landlords prioritise their tenants' needs when making decisions. Businesses prosper when they serve their customers well, and it's no different for landlords.

Being tenant-centric is good for business, and happy tenants may recommend you to other tenants.

A tenant survey conducted by the NRLA in 2024 found that the general landlord-tenant relationship is the main driver of tenant satisfaction, closely followed by maintenance responsiveness. Among dissatisfied tenants, nearly half cited poor responsiveness to maintenance requests as a key issue.[4]

Part of being tenant-centric is being reliable, and doing what you say you'll do, when you say you'll do it. It also means treating tenants with respect and courtesy. Keep the tone of messages and emails professional and respond promptly to their messages.

However, being tenant-centric doesn't mean being a pushover, or agreeing to everything that tenants request. Sometimes their requests are unreasonable. It's best to chat through issues in a friendly but business-like manner to come up with a way forward.

3. Key strategies for landlords

There are two key strategies for private landlords who let direct to tenants: single lets and Houses in Multiple Occupation (HMOs).

Single lets

Single lets are the most straightforward way to let property. The term "single let" refers to letting your entire property to one household, whether that's a family, couple or individual.

They are easier to manage than HMOs, as there are usually no licensing requirements, unless the property is in an area where the local authority requires all landlords to obtain a "selective licence", and there's only one household to deal with.

4. NRLA, *Still Winning – Why Tenants Love Independent Landlords*, 24 January 2024, https://www.nrla.org.uk/research/deep-insight/tenant-survey-autumn24?t.

HMOs

Under section 254 of the Housing Act 2004, Houses in Multiple Occupation (HMOs) are rental properties in which three or more people live, who aren't from the same family, and share facilities such as kitchens and bathrooms. Think student houses or young professional house shares.

The tenants can either have one tenancy agreement for the entire property, called a "joint tenancy", or separate tenancies for each room.

Although HMOs typically attract higher gross yields than single lets, the costs of running HMOs are higher and require significant time, effort and expertise to manage. Being an HMO landlord is not something to take on lightly. Single lets are easier to manage but offer lower returns. Which brings us onto how landlords make money.

Large HMOs with five or more occupants from two or more households need a mandatory licence. In some areas, the local council (also called a local authority) may decide that smaller HMOs need to have an "additional licence" if there are three or four occupants from two or more households. Landlords may also need planning permission to create an HMO, depending on the local council's policy.

HMOs are subject to more stringent legislation, including the Management of Houses in Multiple Occupation (England) Regulations 2006 (HMO Management Regulations), more rigorous fire safety requirements and waste disposal rules. The HMO Management Regulations apply to all section 254 HMOs, even smaller HMOs in areas where they don't need an additional licence.

There is another category of HMOs under section 257 Housing Act 2004 for certain converted flats, which are subject to separate but similar regulations.[5] It is beyond the scope of this book to discuss section 257 HMOs.

4. How do landlords make money?

Being a landlord is a business. Like any business, it needs to generate a return to remain financially viable.

Landlords make money in two ways: rental income and capital growth. We can lose money if our expenses are more than our rental income, or the property goes down in value by the time we want to sell.

According to research by HMRC, in the 2022–23 tax year, 52% of landlords made under £10,000 profit from rental property income, with only 3% of landlords making more than £50,000 in profit.[6]

In this section, I explain the two ways that landlords make money: rental income and capital growth. I also share some useful metrics to help you measure how well your rental business is performing.

Rental income

Rental income is key to being a successful landlord, as it provides the cash flow to cover expenses and generate profit.

---

5. The Licensing and Management of Houses in Multiple Occupation (Additional Provisions) (England) Regulations 2007.
6. *HMRC Research Report no.804: Landlords Research Findings*, (20 May 2025), pp. 18–19, https://www.gov.uk/government/publications/landlords-research.

The rental income is the rent received, before any expenses are deducted.

HMRC figures from the 2022–23 tax year show that the overwhelming majority (79%) of unincorporated landlords in the UK (those who own the property in their own name, rather than through a limited company) earned under £20,000 in gross rental income. Only 4.5% of landlords received more than £50,000 in rental income.[7]

Set the right rent for new tenancies

One of the first decisions that a landlord makes at the start of a tenancy is what the initial rent should be. Although they may take advice from their letting agents, it's the landlord who ultimately decides.

Research the going rent for similar properties in the surrounding area, so that you know what the market rent is for your property. If a property is in good decorative condition, the rent will be higher than a very similar property in a bad state of repair, and it'll be easier to find tenants.

If the rent is too high, it will take longer to let. If they pitch the rent too low, the landlord won't be able to take offers above the asking rent and would need to wait a year before bringing the rent up to the market level.

Rent increases for existing tenants

The average annual rental price inflation across the UK stayed under 2% from March 2017 to January 2022, according to data

7. HM Revenue & Customs, *Property Rental Income Statistics: 2024, Table 13*, https://www.gov.uk/government/statistics/property-rental-income-statistics.

from the Office for National Statistics.[8] During this time, landlords rarely increased the rent for existing tenants and waited to catch up with the market when tenants changed.

However, after a combination of the increases in inflation and interest rates in 2022 and 2023, in-tenancy rent increases became the norm. The Price Index of Private Rents published in January 2026 stated that average rents in England increased by 3.9% in the twelve months to December 2025.[9]

If landlords don't raise rents during periods of inflation, the rent is reducing in real terms. It's better for tenants to have small increases every year than having to cope with a big leap in the rent in one year. Tenants are also more likely to challenge large rent increases, even if the landlord is realigning the rent to the market.

Following the implementation of the tenancy reforms in the RRA, rent review clauses are null and void, and landlords must use the statutory procedure under section 13 of the Housing Act 1988 to increase rent. They also cannot increase rent in the first 12 months of a tenancy, or until at least 12 months have passed since the rent was last increased. I explain the rules further in Chapter 14.

What expenses do landlords have?

Landlords have a lot of running costs and need to budget for them. It's always best to over-estimate how much the

---

8. Office for National Statistics, *Index of Private Housing Rental Prices, UK: January 2022*, https://www.ons.gov.uk/economy/inflationandpriceindices/bulletins/indexofprivatehousingrentalprices/january2022.
9. Office for National Statistics, *Private Rent and House Prices, UK: January 2026*, https://www.ons.gov.uk/economy/inflationandpriceindices/bulletins/privaterentandhousepricesuk/january2026.

expenses are going to be, rather than underestimate, as anything unspent can go in a "rainy day" savings account for future repairs.

Here are the key expenses that landlords incur when running their rental property business:

- financing costs
- letting agent fees
- insurance premiums
- safety and regulatory checks
- repairs and maintenance
- licensing fees
- tax and accounting fees, plus software for Making Tax Digital
- limited company costs
- expenses during voids
- additional costs for leaseholders (e.g. ground rent and service charge)

Financing costs

Unless landlords are cash buyers, they will need to borrow money to finance the purchase. The most popular method is to use an interest-only buy-to-let mortgage at a fixed rate for either a 2- or 5-year period. With interest-only mortgages, landlords aren't repaying any of the capital.

Landlords with a mortgage need to budget to pay the interest each month. The amount will stay the same for the term of the fixed rate. However, as many have found when interest rates suddenly increased to over 5% in 2023 after a long period of historically low rates under 2%, landlords may need to adjust to paying more when the fixed rate period ends.

The tax treatment of the financing costs will depend on whether you own your properties in your own name or through a limited company.

If you own them in your own name (also called an "unincorporated landlord" or a "sole trader landlord"), you are currently only able to get a 20% tax credit for your interest payments for income tax purposes.

On the other hand, if a limited company owns your rental properties, you can offset the full financing costs against corporation tax.

If you're looking for a buy-to-let mortgage, it's important to get help from a mortgage broker who specialises in buy-to-let and isn't tied to one subset of lenders. They'll have access to the whole of the mortgage market and can help you choose the right one for your needs.

Some property investors use bridging finance and/or angel investment, but they're beyond the scope of this book.

Letting agents

Using letting agents to find tenants and manage properties is a major expense for landlords. Full property management costs 8–20% plus VAT of gross rental income, and some agents charge extra for a tenant find.

In London, agents typically charge an on-going percentage of the gross rent for the tenant find, whereas outside of London, it is usually a one-off payment. These costs make a big dent into a landlord's profits.

A large proportion of landlords don't use letting agents. According to the *2024 English Private Landlord Survey*, only 18%

used agents to manage their properties and 43% to find tenants. (These figures understate agent usage as the sample excluded landlords whose agents registered deposits on their behalf, but they confirm that significant numbers of landlords do self-manage.)

Insurance

Landlord insurance

Landlord insurance typically covers the structure of the building against a wide range of risks, from extreme weather to poor electrical or plumbing repairs.

Risks typically covered by landlord insurance:

- Fire and smoke damage
- Flooding and storm damage
- Escape of water
- Freezing of plumbing systems
- Loss of rent (fire/water damage)
- Public liability

Risks typically not covered by landlord insurance:

- General wear and tear
- Insect or bird infestation
- Leaking gutters
- Storm damage to fences or gates

When you call to get a quote for landlord insurance, they'll ask you for the rebuild value of the property, which is the cost to rebuild the property and not the market value.

TIP

If you haven't had a recent valuation, you can look up the rebuild value using the online calculator on the Association of British Insurers' website.[10] Use it to check the rebuild figure your insurance company gives you at renewal.

The freeholder of a leasehold property will typically take out building insurance on behalf of all the leaseholders and charge back the cost through the service charge. However, it's important for leaseholders to check what is and what isn't included in the freeholder's insurance policy. An insurance broker will be able to advise the extent to which you'll need to top it up.

Contents insurance

Contents insurance for landlords covers the contents that belong to the landlord, and not the tenant's belongings.

The price for contents insurance will vary depending on the value of the landlord's items kept within the property and the level and type of cover chosen. Sometimes contents insurance for the landlord's items is covered under landlord insurance.

Let tenants know when they move in that your landlord insurance doesn't cover their contents, so they'll need to take out their own contents insurance.

10. Association of British Insurers, *Calculating Your Rebuild Cost*, https://www.abi.org.uk/products-and-issues/choosing-the-right-insurance/home-insurance/buildings-insurance/calculating-your-rebuild-cost.

Rent guarantee insurance (optional)

Some landlords take out insurance to protect them if their tenant defaults on their rent, which covers missing rent payments and legal fees for eviction. This can be as a stand-alone policy or as an add-on to landlord insurance. As with all insurance, it's important to check the exclusions.

Before you take out rent guarantee insurance, make sure you have followed all the necessary steps for the insurance to be valid, for instance, your tenant's evidence of income and benefits, satisfactory credit history and proof of identity.

Safety and regulatory checks

Landlords incur expenses associated with the following regular safety checks and assessments:

- **Gas Safety Certificate.** An annual Gas Safety Certificate by a Gas Safe Engineer. It's sensible to have the boiler serviced at the same time.
- **Electrical Installation Condition Report (EICR).** This is a report that a qualified electrician will issue after inspecting the electrical installations at a property which states whether or not the electrical installations in the property are satisfactory. It is illegal to let a property to new tenants without a satisfactory EICR, and it usually needs to be redone every five years.
- **Portable appliance testing (PAT testing).** Although it's not strictly a legal requirement for portable appliances to be inspected by an electrician (unless it's a licensing requirement), it's a good idea to do so.

- **Energy Performance Certificate (EPC).** An EPC assesses the energy efficiency of a property on a scale of A–G, with A being the highest. Landlords need to have an EPC from within the last ten years with a rating of E or above before they let a property. This is due to increase to an EPC C in 2030, unless the property has a valid exemption.
- **HMOs.** They have the added cost of fire alarm and emergency lighting testing.

Repairs and maintenance

New landlords often underestimate the number of things that can go wrong with rental properties. Even if margins are tight, it's a false economy not to keep the property in good repair.

A well-maintained property will attract good long-term tenants, and being prompt at fixing things helps keep tenants happy. It also works out cheaper in the long run, as often nipping things in the bud can avoid a greater expense later on. For example, a misaligned down-pipe might cause damp in the house, which would cost more to repair than just realigning the downpipes at the start.

The received wisdom is to budget for at least 10% of the gross rent for repairs and maintenance each year. However, unless the property is a new build or has had a back-to-brick refurbishment, it may well cost more than this. Carpets wear out, boilers need replacing and fittings break, and landlords need to budget for this.

It's a good idea to keep a sinking fund of an additional 10% of the gross rent of all your properties. A sinking fund is a ring-fenced reserve of cash which you build up from a percentage of your rental income, so that if a big expense comes up, like a new roof or replacement windows, you can afford to pay for it, without needing to borrow money.

If your buy-to-let is a flat, you're likely to be contributing through your service charge to the sinking fund held by the freeholder. This means you might not need to put so much aside if it's just to cover expenses for repairs inside the flat. However, you may receive large bills if work is needed for the building.

TIP

Keep a list of trusted tradespersons and service providers you can call upon to handle repairs quickly. Pay their bills promptly, and over time they will value you as a customer.

Licensing

Whilst there isn't an obligation for all rental properties to be licensed in England, there are three potential types of licence that a landlord may be required to obtain. The fees vary considerably from council to council.

I cover licensing in detail in Chapter 5.

TIP

Check to see what discounts are available. For instance, discounts for early renewal or for landlords who are accredited by organisations such as DASH Services,[11]

11. DASH Landlord Accreditation, https://www.dashservices.org.uk/Accreditation.

the London Landlord Accreditation Scheme,[12] or the National Residential Landlords Association (NRLA).[13]

Tax and accountants

I highly recommend paying to have an accountant prepare your tax return and/or company filings. Taxation is complex and it's easy to make a mistake if you're not an accountant yourself. Although I am very much a "do it myself" landlord and know more about tax than the average person, I see it as money well spent to have an accountant do it all for me. The risks that flow from getting it wrong (tax investigation or paying too much tax) outweigh the relatively small cost.

There is also the cost, albeit fairly modest, of Making Tax Digital (MTD) software that started rolling out for unincorporated landlords in April 2026 for those whose annual qualifying income is over £50,000. Landlords have the choice of accounting software, such as Hammock (which I use), or "bridging software" which connects existing spreadsheets to HMRC.

Limited company costs

Landlords who are incorporated, which means they own properties through limited companies, also need to include costs for the company administration and filings at Companies House.[14]

---

12. London Landlord Accreditation Scheme, https://www.londonlandlords.org.uk/accreditation.

13. NRLA Accreditation, https://www.nrla.org.uk/training-academy/accreditation/cpd-activities/accreditation-overview.

14. See this GOV.UK webpage for links to excellent resources: https://www.gov.uk/limited-company-formation.

There are additional costs for incorporated landlords; for instance, the directors need independent legal advice if they provide a personal guarantee when taking out a mortgage or refinancing.

Expenses during voids

When a rental property is unoccupied for any reason (called a void period), the landlord needs to pay expenses that the tenant would ordinarily pay.

These expenses include the following:

Council tax

Many local authorities charge the full council tax when a property is empty, even if it's being refurbished. Some even charge more than the standard council tax for empty properties if they are a second home. Do check with your council and budget for this.

Utilities

The standard tariffs of most utility companies levy standing charges for gas and electricity, which the landlord will need to pay, even if the property is empty. If the property is going to be unoccupied for a lengthy period, it will be worth changing to a tariff without a standing charge.

Landlords should contact their water company if the property is empty, as water companies may suspend charges while a property is empty.

Insurance

Although most landlord insurance allows the property to be unoccupied for a certain period (one to three months), it's important to check how long this period is. It's possible to obtain specialist insurance for unoccupied properties.

Additional costs for leaseholders

Landlords who let flats or leasehold houses will have to pay a service charge and ground rent to the freeholder.

Service charge

While the service charge should include some expenses that a landlord would otherwise pay, such as building insurance and maintenance of the fabric of the building, the level of the service charge is outside of the control of the leaseholders on all but the smallest of developments.

This means that the amount of the service charge can suddenly increase, without warning.

Ground rent

Leaseholders also need to pay ground rent to the freeholder. Whilst for some this is a low or "peppercorn" rent, over the last 30 years or so, many developers have included ground rent clauses that increase the rent in line with inflation or even by doubling the rent a set number of years.

Ground rent was outlawed for new leases granted on or after 30 June 2022 in the Leasehold Reform (Ground Rent) Act 2022.

The Government published the draft Commonhold and Leasehold Bill in January 2026, which contained provisions to cap ground rent at £250 per annum, reducing to a "peppercorn" after 40 years of the implementation of the legislation, for leases entered into before 30 June 2022 at £250 per annum.[15]

Capital growth

In addition to rental income, landlords may also receive a return on their investment if the value of the property increases. This is referred to as capital growth or capital appreciation.

Some landlords make more money through capital growth than they do from rental income. For landlords who own properties for a long time, the capital growth can be considerable, outpacing the Consumer Price Index.

DATA FROM OFFICE OF NATIONAL STATISTICS

2000: the average property in England and Wales cost £84,620, which was the equivalent of approximately £162,205 in 2025, after adjusting for inflation.[16]

December 2025: the average property in England was worth £292,000.[17] This is an increase in value of £207,380 in nominal terms, and approximately

15. Ministry of Housing, Communities and Local Government, *Draft Commonhold and Leasehold Reform Bill.* Policy paper. (2026), https://www.gov.uk/government/publications/draft-commonhold-and-leasehold-reform-bill.

16. April 2000 price (£84,620), Office for National Statistics, *Introducing the Single Official House Price Index,* https://www.ons.gov.uk/releases/introducingthesingleofficialhousepriceindex.

17. Office for National Statistics, *Private Rent and House Prices, UK (18 February*

> £130,000 in real terms, after removing the impact of inflation.[18]

Of course, these figures are just averages, and don't compare apples with apples. However, they show how the value of property can outpace inflation over a 25-year period through capital growth, although the level of capital growth varies considerably between regions. You can find the latest data on the Hometrack website, although it does require a subscription.[19]

Future capital growth invariably won't be the same as in the past. However, it's helpful for landlords to know if a property is in a region where values have risen in the past, to get an understanding of what the total return on the property may be.

Unincorporated landlords pay capital gains tax on the sale of a property that isn't their home, if the total capital gain after deducting the costs of buying, selling and improving the property is more than the annual exempt amount, which is £3,000 for the 2026–27 tax year.[20]

They must also report and pay any capital gains tax due on a property within 60 days of the completion date.

2025), https://www.ons.gov.uk/economy/inflationandpriceindices/datasets/ukhousepriceindexmonthlypricestatistics.

18. Calculated using the Bank of England, *Inflation Calculator*, https://www.bankofengland.co.uk/monetary-policy/inflation/inflation-calculator.

19. See Hometrack: https://www.hometrack.com

20. This web page has the latest rates for capital gains tax: https://www.gov.uk/capital-gains-tax/rates

The amount of tax will depend on whether the landlord is a basic rate taxpayer or a higher rate taxpayer.[21]

Landlords who own their buy-to-let properties via a limited company will pay corporation tax on the chargeable gain on the sale of the property.[22]

Useful metrics for landlords

There are many ways that a landlord can measure the amount of money a buy-to-let makes.

Here are the key metrics:

Yield

Yield is the traditional way of measuring the return an asset generates. It is a useful way of comparing the return of different buy-to-let properties and between different regions. It's historically been higher in the regions with lower historical capital growth.

The yield for a rental property is the gross income a rental property makes in a year, before expenses, as a percentage of its value. This isn't the purchase price, but the current value of the property, so the value will change from year to year.

YIELD: WORKED EXAMPLE

Property value: £200,000

---

21. HM Revenue & Customs, *Tax When you Sell Property*, https://www.gov.uk/tax-sell-property.

22. HM Revenue & Customs, *Corporation Tax When you Sell Business Assets*, https://www.gov.uk/tax-when-your-company-sells-assets.

Annual rent: £12,000

Yield = (£12,000 ÷ £200,000) × 100 = 6%

Return on investment

Return on investment (ROI) measures how well the cash invested in the property is performing. It is calculated as net annual income (gross rent less expenses) divided by the cash invested, expressed as a percentage.

This cash is the deposit the investor used to buy the property, or the amount of cash (also called equity) that is left invested in the property after a refinancing.

Because this metric shows the net income as a percentage of the cash, it will be higher for investments where the mortgage is large, and considerably smaller where the investor owns the property outright without a mortgage.

ROI: WORKED EXAMPLE

Cash invested: £50,000

Annual rent: £12,000

Annual expenses: £4,000

Net annual income = £12,000 - £4,000 = £8,000

ROI = (£8,000 ÷ £50,000) × 100 = 16%

Net cash flow

Net cash flow is rental income minus expenses (including any mortgage). A positive cash flow means the property is paying its way; a negative cash flow means you're subsidising it from other income.

Rent arrears can also push cash flow negative.

NET CASH FLOW: WORKED EXAMPLE

Monthly rent: £1,000

Monthly expenses: £700

Net monthly cash flow before tax = £1,000 - £700 = £300

Net profit

Net profit after tax is the bottom line, which is the figure that landlords should use to assess if their buy-to-let is making money from rental income.

NET PROFIT: WORKED EXAMPLE

Annual income: £12,000

Annual expenses: £8,000

Net profit before tax = £12,000 - £8,000 = £4,000

Assumption of income tax of £1,500

Net profit after tax = £4,000 - £1,500 = £2,500

5. Record-keeping and administration

Whether you own one property or 100, you need to keep proper records for tax purposes, to prove compliance with your legal obligations and to protect yourself in any dispute.

This means:

- A separate bank account for your property income and expenses.
- Organised storage of invoices, receipts, safety certificates and tenancy documents (see Chapter 11 for more tips).
- Records of communications with tenants and agents.

Also, landlords who own properties through a limited company must file relevant documents with Companies House and comply with the standard requirements for displaying the company name on correspondence and at business premises. Tenancy agreements and any licences must be in the company's name and not the landlord's personal name.

Now we've explored the business of being a landlord, we move on to an overview of the key points of the Renters' Rights Act 2025, which is the topic for Chapter 2.

CHAPTER 2

RENTERS' RIGHTS ACT 2025 OVERVIEW

Although I have integrated the provisions of the Renters' Rights Act 2025 (RRA) into every chapter of this book, this stand-alone chapter runs through the key changes it introduced.

1. The new assured periodic tenancy

All assured shorthold tenancies that were in place on 1 May 2026, whether they were in a fixed-term period or already periodic, automatically converted into assured periodic tenancies on that day.

The assured periodic tenancy is now the default tenancy in England, and it has not been possible to create a new assured shorthold tenancy since 30 April 2026.

What is an assured periodic tenancy?

A tenancy will be classified as an assured periodic tenancy by the Housing Act 1988[1] if each of the following apply:

- The tenant is one or more individuals (not a company).

1. See Part I of Schedule 1 of the Housing Act 1988.

- The tenant occupies the property as their "only or principal home".
- The tenant has exclusive possession, and has the right to refuse entry to anyone, including the landlord, except in an emergency.
- The landlord does not live in the property (i.e., it is not a lodger arrangement where the tenant shares facilities with a resident landlord).
- It is not a high rent tenancy, i.e. the annual rent is not over £100,000.
- It is not a low rent tenancy, i.e. the annual rent is more than £1,000 in London and £250 outside of London.
- It is not a tenancy regulated by the Rent Act 1977.
- It is not purpose-built student accommodation, which falls within the exemption under section 32 RRA.

Tenancies that are not governed by the Housing Act 1988, for instance high rent tenancies, are known as "Non-Housing Act" tenancies, or NHA.

JESSICA, PAUL AND DEBORAH

Jessica owns a flat and lets the spare room to Olivia, and they share the kitchen and the bathroom. This is not an assured periodic tenancy, as Jessica is a resident landlord and Olivia is a lodger.

Paul inherited a house in Notting Hill which he lets to a family for £2,000 per week. This is not an assured periodic tenancy as the annual rent is more than £100,000, also called a "high rent tenancy", which is outside the Housing Act 1988.

Deborah owns a nice house in Didsbury, Manchester, which she lets to five professionals to live in, for £800 per room per month including bills.

This is an assured periodic tenancy as the tenants have exclusive possession of their rooms, and it's their sole or main home. It's also a house in multiple occupation (HMO) as there are more than three people from two separate households sharing the kitchen and other common parts.

Tenant's right to serve notice to quit

As mentioned in the Introduction, Housing Act tenancies are now all periodic and can no longer have a fixed-term period.

There is also no minimum period for a tenancy, and a tenant has the right to terminate the tenancy at any time by serving two months' notice to quit to expire at the end of a rent period or the following day.

This period can be shorter if the agreement has a shorter notice period, such as one calendar month.

If a tenancy was still in a fixed-term period on 1 May 2026, the fixed term ended immediately, and the tenancy became periodic, by operation of law.

EMILY

Emily rents a room in Deborah's HMO, and the rent period runs from the 2nd of the month to the 1st of the month.

Emily wants to leave, and serves Deborah notice to quit on 10 June. As she needs to give two months' notice to expire in line with the rent period, a notice to quit cannot terminate the tenancy until 1 September at the earliest.

It cannot validly expire on 10 August as the expiry of the notice must align with her rent period.

Since her rent period runs from the 2nd to the 1st, the notice must expire on the 1st of a month or the 2nd. The first "1st of the month" that occurs after 10 August is 1 September. Consequently, Emily is liable for the rent for the entire final rent period from 2 August to 1 September (or 2 September if her notice expires then).

Fixed term ban

Landlords must not "purport to let" a property for a fixed term from 1 May 2026, for instance by accidentally using an old AST with a fixed term. This is because the local council may impose a civil penalty on the landlord of up to £7,000 if they are satisfied beyond reasonable doubt that the landlord has breached this rule.

Any term of a tenancy agreement which states that the tenancy is a fixed term is null and void.

TIP

Make sure you do not use an assured shorthold tenancy agreement when you sign up new tenants. Instead, use a template that has been created for the new assured periodic tenancy in the RRA. See Appendix 1: Further resources for more details.

Provision of written statement of terms

Section 12 RRA introduced a requirement for landlords to provide tenants with a "written statement" that sets out the terms of the tenancy and certain other information before the tenant enters into the tenancy.

This means that landlords can no longer have an informal, oral arrangement with tenants, and must give them a document which sets out the terms of the tenancy before they enter into the tenancy.

The details are set out in the Written Statement etc Regulations,[2] which I go into in more detail in Chapter 9.

In practice, the written statement is included as part of the assured periodic tenancy agreement, although it can be in a separate document. Tenants must be given the opportunity to read it before they sign it.

A landlord can receive a civil penalty of up to £7,000 if the local housing authority is satisfied beyond reasonable doubt that the landlord breached this obligation.

For recommendations of providers of template documentation, see Appendix 1: Further resources.

Abolition of section 21

The RRA abolished assured shorthold tenancies by removing Chapter 2 of Part 1 from the Housing Act 1988, which contained the rules for assured shorthold tenancies. This included section 21, which gave landlords the right to recover

2. The Assured Tenancies (Private Rented Sector) (Written Statement of Terms etc and Information Sheet) (England) Regulations 2026.

possession by giving two months' notice to the tenant via a so-called "no fault eviction" notice.

Any clause in a tenancy agreement that attempts to give the landlord the right to terminate an assured periodic tenancy agreement with two months' notice is null and void. Also, if the landlord attempts to serve a notice to quit or even ask the tenants to leave, the local council may impose a civil penalty of up to £7,000.

The only way for landlords to terminate an assured periodic tenancy is if they have a valid reason under section 8 of the Housing Act 1988 and follow the statutory process.

The key revamped section 8 grounds for possession

The RRA removed the flexibility that section 21 gave landlords to terminate a tenancy without giving a reason. Under the new regime, landlords can only bring a tenancy to an end if they serve a notice under section 8 of the Housing Act, relying on a statutory reason, called a "ground for possession". These grounds are set out in Schedule 2 of the Housing Act 1988.

However, the RRA introduced new and amended grounds for possession under section 8 which give landlords a certain measure of flexibility, albeit less than that under section 21.

I go into the grounds in detail in Chapter 15, but these are the key grounds for possession:

- Ground 1A: landlord selling up
- Ground 1: landlord moving in
- Ground 4A: full time students in HMO
- Ground 8: serious rent arrears

- Grounds 7A and 14: anti-social behaviour
- Ground 12: breach of tenancy agreement.

2. Changes to the rules about rent

The RRA introduced a lot of changes relating to rent, and here's an overview of the changes:

- Landlords must include the proposed rent in any listing and cannot let the property for more than this amount, even if a tenant offers to pay more.
- Landlords cannot ask tenants to pay any rent before the tenancy agreement is entered into. They also cannot accept any rent payments before the tenancy is entered into.
- Any term in a tenancy agreement entered into on or after 1 May 2026 that says that more than one month's rent is payable at any one time is invalid.
- The only way to increase rent once a tenant has moved in is to use a statutory process, which involves serving on the tenant a prescribed form that proposes the new rent, called Form 4A,[3] at least two months before the new rent is due to start.
- Tenants can challenge all proposed rent increases in the First-tier Tribunal.
- Landlords cannot agree a new rent informally with their tenants, unless the landlord first serves Form 4A. Rent review clauses in tenancy agreements are null and void. The next rent increase cannot be for another 12 months after the new rent comes into force.

3. Form 4A is available on this web page: https://www.gov.uk/guidance/assured-tenancy-forms

For more details, see Chapter 14: Rent.

3. Right for tenants to keep pets

Tenants have the right to keep a pet, so long as they follow the statutory procedure to ask the landlord for permission, and the landlord in fact gives permission.

The landlord cannot refuse a request unless they have a good reason, which in the case of leasehold properties can include a ban in the lease or if the freeholder refuses to give consent.

Landlords also cannot insist that the tenants take out insurance for pet damage or charge the tenant for their own costs of taking out insurance against pet damage, as that would be a breach of the Tenant Fees Act 2019.

The original version of the Renters' Rights Bill had wording that would have enabled landlords to insist on pet damage insurance, but that was later removed by the Government before the bill became law.

For more details, see Chapter 12.

4. Rental discrimination

Chapter 3 of Part 1 of the RRA makes it illegal for landlords and agents to have blanket bans on renting to people who receive benefits or who have children. This is referred to as "rental discrimination".

Landlords and letting agents must not prevent anyone from enquiring about renting a property, viewing the property, or entering into a tenancy agreement on the basis that they have a child who would live or visit there and/or they are a benefits claimant.

However, the landlord or agent can take a person's income (including benefits) into account when assessing affordability. They can also consider whether the property would be suitable for children, if it's a "proportionate means of achieving a legitimate aim", such as to avoid overcrowding.

The RRA extends the prohibition to lease agreements, mortgages and insurance contracts, by saying that any term in a contract that prohibits landlords from letting to families or tenants on benefits has "no effect".

Landlords can still choose whether to let to people who receive benefits or who have children, but they can't automatically turn down families or those on benefits.

The rental discrimination rules ban overt discrimination, for instance "No DSS" advertisements. They also ban indirect discrimination, which makes it more difficult for families and those who receive benefits to rent a suitable property.

Councils can impose financial penalties on a landlord or a letting agent if they are satisfied on a balance of probabilities that there has been a breach of the rules on rental discrimination, i.e. it's more likely than not to be true.

BOB AND JOSH, PART 1

Bob, a landlord, tells his letting agent, Josh, that he won't consider any applicants who receive any form of benefits, even if they can afford the rent and have a good credit history. Josh screens out all applicants who receive benefits and refuses to let them view the property. This is rental discrimination. (Part 2 follows below).

5. Private Rented Sector Database

Once it is fully in force, every landlord and every residential property will need to have an active entry on the new Private Rented Sector Database (Database) before they can market a property or offer a property for rent. This will make it easier for prospective tenants and local authorities to look up information on landlords and rental properties.

Councils will be able to issue civil penalties for up to £7,000 if a landlord breaches the rules, and up to £40,000 for providing false or misleading information to the Database, or for a continuing breach of the obligation not to let a property without having active entries on the Database for the landlord and the property.

Also, tenants will be able to apply to the First-tier Tribunal for a rent repayment order if the landlord provides false or misleading information to the Database, or either repeats a breach or continues a breach after receiving a civil penalty.

At the time of writing, the Database is not yet live, and we do not have the details of what information will need to go in the Database.

The Government's *Implementation Roadmap* published in November 2025, referred to the Database starting to roll out "from late 2026", and registration is expected to become mandatory in 2027.[4]

---

4. Ministry of Housing, Communities and Local Government, *Implementing the Renters' Rights Act 2025: Our Roadmap for Reforming the Private Rented Sector,*

6. Private Rented Sector Landlord Ombudsman

After launch, all private landlords must join the Private Rented Sector Landlord Ombudsman scheme (Ombudsman), regardless of whether they use a letting agent.

The Ombudsman will have the power to require landlords to make an apology, provide information, take remedial action and/or pay compensation. Landlords will also be obliged to comply with the Ombudsman's decisions.

Councils will be able to impose a civil penalty on a landlord of up to £7,000 for a first breach of the obligation to join the Ombudsman scheme, or if they continue the breach. This can increase up to £40,000 for serious, persistent, or repeated violations.

As of the date of publication, the Ombudsman has not yet been launched, but the *Implementation Roadmap*[5] referred to landlords being required to be members of the Ombudsman scheme in 2028.

7. Property condition

Decent Homes Standard

The Decent Homes Standard (DHS) was originally introduced for social housing in 2001 and was last updated in 2006. Its

Policy paper (November 2025), https://www.gov.uk/government/publications/renters-rights-act-2025-implementation-roadmap.

5. MHCLG, *Implementation Roadmap* (2025).

purpose is to ensure that social housing homes are safe, in good repair and have modern facilities.[6]

The Renters' Rights Act introduced a requirement for properties in the private rented sector, including HMOs, which are let under an assured periodic tenancy or the Rent Act 1977 to meet certain minimum standards, to be set out by the Secretary of State in regulations.

The Secretary of State also has the power to extend the DHS to licences to occupy and other types of tenancies (such as high rent tenancies) by regulation.

The Government announced in January 2026 that it will come into force 2035.[7]

Awaab's Law

Awaab's Law is named after Awaab Ishak, the toddler who died in 2020 because of "a severe respiratory condition due to prolonged exposure to mould in his home environment", to use the words of the coroner in her report.[8] This home was social housing, run by Rochdale Boroughwide Housing.

This led to an amendment to section 10 of the Landlord and

6. Department for Communities and Local Government, *A Decent Home: Definition and Guidance for Implementation* (June 2006), https://assets.publishing.service.gov.uk/government/uploads/system/uploads/attachment_data/file/7812/138355.pdf.

7. Ministry of Housing, Communities and Local Government, *The New Decent Homes Standard: Policy Statement* (January 2026), https://www.gov.uk/government/consultations/consultation-on-a-reformed-decent-homes-standard-for-social-and-privately-rented-homes/outcome/the-new-decent-homes-standard-policy-statement.

8. Courts and Tribunals Judiciary, *Awaab Ishak – Prevention of Future Deaths* (16 September 2022), https://www.judiciary.uk/prevention-of-future-death-reports/awaab-ishak-prevention-of-future-deaths-report/.

Tenant Act 1985, introduced for social housing by the Social Housing (Regulation) Act 2023, which requires social landlords to take action in relation to certain prescribed hazards, including damp and mould.

The RRA extends this obligation to the private rented sector, although as of the date of publication, this has not been implemented. The *Implementation Roadmap* states that MHCLG would "consult on the details of this policy, including implementation timescales, in due course".[9]

8. Local authorities' investigatory powers

Chapter 3 of Part 4 of the RRA significantly extended the ability of local councils to obtain information, enter premises and investigate offences under housing law. These powers came into force on 27 December 2025.

Power to require documents

Councils have the power to require anyone to provide information and documents if the relevant council officer wishes to investigate a suspected breach of rented accommodation legislation (see below).

These include the rules regarding rental discrimination, HMO and selective licensing, and, once launched, the PRS Ombudsman and the PRS Landlord Database.

9. Ministry of Housing, Communities and Local Government, *DHS Consultation* (2025).

Right to enter certain business premises

Councils also have the right to enter business premises without a warrant of someone in the rental sector business, for instance a letting agent, if a council officer:

- "reasonably suspects" a breach of or an offence under rented accommodation legislation, and
- considers it necessary to enter the premises to seize documents or demand documents to enable them to decide whether there has been compliance with the rented accommodation legislation.

Rented accommodation legislation

Councils have powers to investigate suspected breaches of this rented accommodation legislation:

- **Sections 1 and 1A of the Protection from Eviction Act 1977:** Harassment and illegal eviction.
- **Chapter 1 of Part 1 of the Housing Act 1988:** Assured tenancy rules, security of tenure, orders for possession, rent increases.
- **Chapter 3 of Part 1 of the Renters' Rights Act 2025:** Rental discrimination.
- **Part 2 of the Renters' Rights Act 2025:** Landlord Redress Scheme and PRS Database.
- **Parts 1–4 and 7 of the Housing Act 2004:** HHSRS, HMO licensing, selective licensing.
- **Section 83(1) or 84(1) of the Enterprise and Regulatory Reform Act 2013:** publication of letting agent fees, membership of letting agent redress scheme.

- **Sections 21–23 of the Housing and Planning Act 2016:** Breach of banning order, offences by companies and those committed with the consent, connivance or neglect of a director, manager, etc.

Additional offences

The investigatory powers of local councils have real teeth, as it's an offence for someone not to comply with a request to provide information and documentation, unless they have a "reasonable excuse" not to.

It's also an offence for someone to make a statement to a council officer which they know to be "false or misleading in a material respect", or "recklessly" make a statement which is materially false or misleading.

Anyone found guilty of one of these offences is liable on summary conviction (i.e. in a Magistrates' Court) to a fine of up to level 3 on the standard scale, which is currently £1,000.[10]

This is on top of any other sanctions that the council, tribunal or courts impose.

9. Sanctions

Landlords potentially face three different types of sanctions if they breach certain duties or commit offences.

There are civil penalties for breaches of many landlord obligations, and if the breach is also an offence, the council can

10. See Sentencing Council, *Fine Calculator*, https://www.sentencingcouncil.org.uk/fine-calculator/.

either bring a criminal prosecution or impose a civil penalty, and the First-tier Tribunal may impose a rent repayment order.

Civil penalties

The RRA gives councils the power to impose civil penalties on landlords and letting agents who breach most of the new duties and obligations.

For an initial breach, such as discriminating against tenants because they receive benefits, a civil penalty may be up to £7,000. In cases of offences, for instance, repeated breaches or unlawful eviction, the civil penalty may increase to up to £40,000 as an alternative to prosecution.

Statutory guidance sets out the factors local authorities should consider when developing their civil penalty policy to ensure that penalties are set at an appropriate level, and the starting point for each breach and offence.[11] As an example, the starting point for attempting to let a property for a fixed term in breach of the new section 16E(1)(a) of the Housing Act 1988 is £4,000.

What proof does the council need?

In most cases, the council needs to be satisfied "beyond reasonable doubt" that a landlord or other relevant person such as a letting agent has breached the law before it can impose a civil penalty. This is the same standard as for criminal law.

11. Ministry of Housing, Communities and Local Government (2025) *Civil Penalties Under the Renters' Rights Act 2025 and Other Housing Legislation.* Statutory guidance. https://www.gov.uk/government/publications/civil-penalties-under-the-renters-rights-act-2025-and-other-housing-legislation.

However, the standard is lower for the obligations to state the proposed rent, not to engage in rental bidding and rental discrimination, as the local council merely needs to be satisfied on a "balance of probabilities", i.e. it's more likely than not to be true.

Examples of duties

Here is a list of the key duties in the Renters' Rights Act where local authorities can impose a civil penalty if they are satisfied that there has been a breach by a landlord or another relevant person:

- Duty not to purport to let for a fixed term
- Duty to state the proposed rent
- No rental bidding
- No rental discrimination
- Prohibited pre-tenancy rent payment
- Duty not to knowingly or recklessly misuse possession grounds
- Obligation not to re-let or market the property for let during a restricted period

A full list of the civil penalties introduced or amended in the Renters' Rights Act are set out in Appendix 3. I also explain the duties in the relevant chapters.

BOB AND JOSH, PART 2

When Bob told Josh he didn't want anyone on benefits viewing the property, Josh added a note to the agency's software: "Bob says no DSS", and systematically screened out anyone receiving benefits.

Joanna applied to view the property and was turned down, despite having an excellent credit record, a steady job and good references. As she received Universal Credit, she suspected this was the reason and complained to the council.

The council officer asked the branch manager for access to the software and the benefit status of each applicant who had viewed the property. Not a single applicant receiving benefits had been allowed to view, and the officer found Josh's note: "Bob says no DSS".

This was enough for the council to be satisfied, on a balance of probabilities, that both Bob and Josh had broken the rules banning rental discrimination. Both received a civil penalty, with Bob's being higher as it was not his first offence.

The procedure for issuing civil penalties

Before issuing a civil penalty, the council must give the relevant person a notice of intent which includes the amount of the penalty, the reasons for proposing to impose a penalty and information about the right to make representations. (Note that the council must also act in accordance with their civil penalty policy.)

The landlord or agent will have the right to put their side of the case to the council by making "written representations" to the council within 28 days of receiving the notice of intent.

If the council wishes to impose the penalty after this 28-day period ends, they must give a final notice to the person, which includes the amount of the penalty, the reasons for imposing it, when and how it is payable and their rights of appeal.

Rights to appeal against civil penalty

If someone receives a civil penalty from the council, they will have 28 days to appeal to the First-tier Tribunal against both the decision to impose the penalty and the amount of the penalty.

Criminal prosecution

The RRA introduced several new criminal offences for which landlords may be prosecuted in the Magistrates' Court, most with a maximum penalty on conviction of an unlimited fine.

Here are the new criminal offences in the Renters' Rights Act , which all attract a potentially unlimited fine on conviction:

- Persistent failure to join Landlord Ombudsman
- Persistent failure to join PRS Database
- Knowingly or recklessly providing false information to PRS Database
- Knowingly misusing a possession ground (section 8 Housing Act 1988)
- Re-letting or marketing for re-letting within restricted period after using "selling up" and "moving in" grounds 1A and 1
- Continued or repeated breach of duties in sections 16D and 16E of the Housing Act 1988 after receiving civil penalty

The council has the option to impose a civil penalty for these offences, as an alternative to criminal prosecution.

Also, tenants and councils can apply to the First-tier Tribunal for a rent repayment order if a landlord commits any of these offences.

Rent repayment orders

The Housing Act 2004, as amended by the Housing and Planning Act 2016, previously gave tenants and local authorities the right to reclaim up to 12 months of rent from landlords who committed specific offences. This is called a "rent repayment order".

Section 98 of the Renters' Rights Act strengthened the ability for tenants and local authorities to apply for rent repayment orders to increase the deterrent effect and make it "more appealing" for tenants and local authorities to pursue. It's part of "tenant-led enforcement".[12]

Tenants can apply to the First-tier Tribunal for the repayment of up to two years' rent. However, if part of the rent was paid through Housing Benefit or Universal Credit, the local authority can claim a rent repayment order in respect of that rent paid through public funds.

How the Renters' Rights Act changes rent repayment orders

Sections 103 and 104 of the RRA extend liability to superior landlords (including freeholders) and company directors and double the maximum award from 12 to 24 months' rent.

---

12. Quotes from Ministry of Housing, Communities and Local Government, *Guide to the Renters' Rights Act* (6 November 2025), https://www.gov.uk/government/publications/guide-to-the-renters-rights-act/guide-to-the-renters-rights-act#rent-repayment-orders.

As liability extends to superior landlords, if a superior landlord leases a property to a "guaranteed rent" provider or other intermediary who then sub-lets it, and the superior landlord commits an offence, the superior landlord will still be liable, even though they are not the direct landlord of the tenants.

In other words, landlords cannot hide behind an intermediary.

Local authorities and tenants now have two years to apply for a rent repayment order, whereas previously it was just one year.

List of offences

Here is the full list of offences that can lead to a rent repayment order, including those introduced by the Renters' Rights Act:

- Violence for securing entry.
- Unlawful eviction or harassment of tenants.
- Failing to comply with an improvement notice.
- Failing to comply with a prohibition order.
- Control or management of an unlicensed HMO.
- Control or management of an unlicensed house.
- Breach of banning order.
- Knowingly or recklessly misusing a possession ground.
- Breach of restriction on letting or marketing a dwelling-house.
- Tenancy reform: continuing breaches.
- PRS Landlord Ombudsman: continuing or repeat breaches.
- PRS Database: provision of false or misleading information.
- PRS Database: continuing or repeat breaches.

Having looked at the specific areas where Renters' Rights Act has changed landlords' obligations, we will now step back and look at the key obligations of landlords in the round in Chapter 3.

CHAPTER 3

KEY LEGAL OBLIGATIONS FOR LANDLORDS

The private rented sector is heavily regulated, and the Renters' Rights Act introduced another swathe of regulation.

To make matters particularly challenging for landlords, there isn't a single point of reference that landlords can look up. Instead, there are layers upon layers of statutes, regulations and guidance, which can be difficult to navigate.

Some statutes are overarching, like the Housing Act 1988 (HA88), which is the key source of the current rights and obligations of landlords and tenants in the PRS. This has been amended by many other statutes, not least the Renters' Rights Act 2025 (RRA).

Other statutes are more specific, such as the Tenant Fees Act 2019 (TFA), which prohibits landlords and letting agents from charging tenants a wide range of fees.

Secondary legislation is another important source of legal obligations for landlords. This is law created by government ministers (or other bodies) under powers given to them by an Act of Parliament (called primary legislation) in the form of regulations or orders. For instance, the Electrical Safety Standards in the Private Rented Sector (England) Regulations 2020 introduced the obligation for landlords to obtain an EICR (Electrical Installation Condition Report) at least every 5 years.

Many regulations implement different provisions in the Renters' Rights Act.

You can find links to the primary and secondary legislation that I refer to in this handbook in Appendix 2: Legislation.

In this chapter, I go through each of the key legal obligations for landlords, including those which the RRA introduced.

1. Responsibilities for repair and maintenance

The basic rule is that landlords must look after their properties and keep them safe and in good repair, so they're fit for people to live in.

Here are the specific responsibilities that landlords have, together with the relevant legislation:

Repair the structure and exterior

Under section 11 of the Landlord and Tenant Act 1985 (LTA), landlords must carry out repairs to the roof, drains, gutters, external pipes, windows and exterior doors and main access to the property. This includes fences, gates and garden sheds. Garden maintenance, by contrast, is the tenant's responsibility unless the tenancy agreement provides otherwise (for instance, if the rent includes the services of a gardener in an HMO).

This obligation extends to the common parts that the landlord is responsible for, for instance, if the landlord is also the freeholder of a block of flats. Landlords often overlook gutters and downpipes. Although it may seem trivial, dripping water can do significant damage to the brickwork, leading to damp and mould.

Keep gas, electrical, plumbing and water installations in good repair

The LTA requires landlords to keep in repair and proper working order the installations for the supply of water, gas, electricity, sanitation, heating and hot water. This means that the landlord is responsible for ensuring that the basins, sinks, baths, showers, toilets, the boiler and the central heating system work properly.

Landlords should also provide safety operating instructions for the boiler and all electrical equipment and appliances. They should also show tenants where the stopcocks and isolator switches are located when they move in and include this in a property manual in case they forget.

Ensure the property is fit for human habitation

Section 9A of the Landlord and Tenant Act 1985 requires landlords to ensure that their rental properties are fit for human habitation, both at the start of and throughout the tenancy, so that the properties are safe, healthy and suitable for someone to live in. It establishes a baseline standard for tenants.

For a property to be considered unfit for human habitation, it must be so defective in one or more specific matters to render it as not reasonably suitable for someone to live there in that condition. These matters include repair, stability, freedom from damp, internal layout, natural lighting, ventilation, water supply, drainage and facilities for food preparation.

Landlords must also make sure there are no serious hazards that could pose a risk to health or safety, such as dangerous stairs, exposed wiring or issues like mould linked to poor ventilation.

Housing Health and Safety Rating System (HHSRS)

The Housing Act 2004 obliges local authorities to keep the housing conditions in their area under review, using the Housing Health and Safety Rating System (HHSRS) to identify potential hazards and evaluate the potential risk of harm.

The HHSRS was overhauled in 2026, when new statutory guidance simplified the system.

There are now 21 individual potential hazards, ranging from damp and mould growth to excess cold and inadequate lighting.

HHSRS assessments categorise hazards into two categories:

- Category 1 hazards – these pose an imminent risk to health.
- Category 2 hazards – these are serious hazards but are unlikely to cause direct harm in the near future.

Local authorities must take action against the landlord if they identify Category 1 hazards. They can also decide to take action for Category 2 hazards if they believe it's appropriate.

The HHSRS rules also need to be read alongside both the Decent Homes Standard and Awaab's Law, which the RRA will extend to the private rented sector when they are eventually implemented.

How quickly must landlords carry out repairs?

Landlords should carry out repairs within a "reasonable time" from when the tenant reports the problem. The law doesn't define how long a reasonable time is, and it will depend on how urgent the problem is and the time of year.

If a gas boiler breaks, the landlord (or their agent) should organise for a qualified gas boiler engineer to visit the property to repair the boiler as soon as possible, say the same day or the next. A plumber should attend the same or following day if there is a burst water pipe, as well as the tenant turning off the stopcock to prevent further damage. If the central heating isn't working in the middle of winter, that is more urgent than if it breaks in summer.

Some issues take time to fix, and tradespersons might not be available straight away. For instance, if a window needs replacing, there is usually a lead time of around two months to order a new one of the correct size. (Windows might seem to be a standard size, but they're not.) The landlord may choose to leave some minor issues until later, if they aren't a "hazard" for HHSRS purposes and are not urgent. However, the delay must be reasonable.

Landlords will eventually have specific timeframes to remedy hazards under Awaab's Law. At the time of publication, the specific details and timescales remain subject to consultation.

Access to the property for repairs

Section 11 of the Landlord and Tenant Act 1985 inserts an implied covenant into all tenancy agreements that the landlord or their authorised representative may enter the property at reasonable times of the day to view their "condition and state of repair" by giving 24 hours' written notice to the tenant. Tenancy agreements usually contain an explicit term to this effect as well.

However, this obligation on the tenant is subject to the tenant's right of quiet enjoyment of their home. Consequently, landlords cannot enter the property without the tenant's permission.

If a tenant refuses entry for pre-arranged repairs or a Gas Safety Certificate, you cannot force entry. While you may be able to claim wasted call-out from the contractor for the missed appointment, you must respect their right to refuse access unless it's a genuine emergency, such as a suspected gas leak, water leak or where a serious hazard poses a risk of injury.

What tenants are responsible for maintaining

Tenants are required to behave in a "tenant-like manner", which means they should take care of the property. Under section 9A of the Landlord and Tenant Act 1985, a landlord isn't required to repair the damage caused by tenants.

Here are some examples of what tenants, and not landlords, are responsible for doing:

- Changing light bulbs and fuses.
- Keeping the inside and outside of the property clean.
- Disposing of rubbish in the bins provided and putting the appropriate bin out for collection on bin day.
- Unblocking sinks, baths and showers. This includes clearing out hair from the traps in showers and baths.

- Not flushing wet wipes, nappies or sanitary products down the toilet – this can cause blockages in the drains and lead to flooding.
- Keeping the toilet and appliances free of limescale using appropriate products.
- Bleeding radiators and resetting the pressure of the boiler when needed.
- Maintaining the garden, including lawn mowing and sweeping leaves, unless the tenancy agreement says the landlord will arrange this.
- Cleaning bathrooms and kitchens and keeping them free of mould.
- Keeping windows condensation-free – this means opening windows and using any extractor fans to air the room and prevent mould.

Tenants must also pay to repair damage that they or their guests cause. For instance, from an over-flowing bath or a flood from a shower tray due to hair in the plug hole, or wet wipes blocking the waste.

2. Safety obligations

Landlords are subject to the following rules regarding the safety of rental properties:

Gas safety

Landlords have a legal obligation to ensure that all gas appliances (such as the boiler, hob and oven), fittings and flues are adequately maintained. This includes arranging for a Gas

Safe Engineer[1] to carry out an annual gas safety inspection for every gas appliance (such as boilers, hobs and gas fires) and related fittings and flues, and obtain a satisfactory CP12 certificate, also called a Gas Safety Certificate.

It's advisable but not strictly an obligation to have the boiler serviced.

Once the checks have been performed, the landlord will receive a copy of the CP12 certificate from the engineer. It's important that the Gas Safe Engineer signs the certificate as an attestation of accuracy.

Landlords must provide the Gas Safety Certificate to tenants before they move in and within 28 days of any follow-up check. Failing to provide the CP12 form is a criminal offence, and landlords can face civil penalties of up to £6,000 or 6 months in prison for not doing this.

Under the old section 21 rules, a valid Gas Safety Certificate was a prerequisite for eviction. Although landlords have a legal obligation to provide a valid safety certificate to tenants each year, failure to do so does not prevent a possession under section 8.

This means that landlords can use a section 8 notice to evict a tenant, even if they did not obtain a Gas Safety Certificate before the start of or during the tenancy.

TIP

Keep copies of all Gas Safety Certificates and a record of

1. You can check the Gas Safe Register to see if someone is legally entitled to carry out the Gas Safety Certificate on this webpage: https://www.gassaferegister.co.uk/find-an-engineer-or-check-the-register.

when they were provided to the tenants. Diarise a reminder two months before each Gas Safety Certificate is due to expire.

Like MOTs, landlords can get a Gas Safety Certificate done up to two months beforehand and still keep the original expiry date.

Electrical Installation Condition Report (EICR)

The Electrical Safety Standards in the Private Rented Sector (England) Regulations 2020 require landlords in England to arrange for a "qualified and competent person" to inspect and test the electrical installations in rental properties at least every five years.

The inspection checks whether any electrical installations are overloaded and whether there are any potential electric shock risks and fire hazards. It also looks for any defective electrical work or a lack of earthing or bonding (which prevent electric shocks).

The electrician will issue an Electrical Installation Condition Report (EICR), which states whether the condition of the installations is satisfactory or unsatisfactory.

If the condition is unsatisfactory, the report will identify any damage, deterioration, defects and/or potentially dangerous conditions, with detailed recommendations about remedial works. The landlord must ensure that the required remedial work or further investigation is carried out within 28 days of the unsatisfactory EICR, or a shorter period if stated in the report.

The landlord must provide any existing tenants with a copy of the EICR within 28 days of the testing. This is the case regardless of whether the EICR is satisfactory or unsatisfactory.

When a landlord is preparing a property to let, and the EICR is due to expire before the tenants move in (or there isn't an EICR), they should arrange it as soon as possible. This is because it's illegal for tenants to move into the property unless it has a satisfactory EICR.

Consequently, if the EICR is unsatisfactory, the remedial works must be completed before the tenants can move into the property.

TIP

Put a recurring reminder in your calendar or property management software for the date when the EICR is due to expire so you don't miss it, with a reminder a month before. Five years can pass quickly, so a calendar reminder is helpful!

Portable appliance testing (PAT testing)

Portable appliances are electrical appliances that connect to the mains via a plug and can be relocated. For instance, small appliances such as kettles and toasters, as well as larger appliances such as washing machines and dishwashers.

If landlords provide portable appliances, they should be safe for tenants to use. Although it's not a legal requirement to pay an electrician to test portable appliances, as the landlord may do a visual inspection, many landlords prefer the peace of mind of paying for annual PAT testing by an electrician.

Formal PAT testing should be done by a qualified electrician who will carry out a visual inspection of the appliance, its plug and lead. For those appliances with an earth (Class I), they will also test the cable and the appliance itself.

For landlords carrying out the PAT testing themselves, they should carry out a visual inspection of each portable appliance once a year and check the following:

- Is the plug in good condition – is there any tape to join it to the lead and are there signs of overheating?
- Is the lead in good condition, without fraying, cuts or signs of excessive wear?
- Is the appliance stored somewhere wet or damp?
- Whilst not "visual", does the plug smell when turned on?

Smoke alarms

Smoke alarms must be fitted on every floor with living accommodation and tested every year. They can be battery operated for single lets, but must be hard-wired and interlinked for licensed HMOs, with weekly testing for large HMOs.[2]

Landlords should arrange for the testing of smoke alarms at the start of a tenancy, and tenants should test them each year. That said, it's easy to ask the gas engineer to check the smoke alarms when they do the Gas Safety Certificate.

---

2. See LACoRS, *Housing Fire Safety Guidance* for more information: https://www.cieh.org/media/1244/guidance-on-fire-safety-provisions-for-certain-types-of-existing-housing.pdf.

Carbon monoxide alarms

Any room with a fuel-burning appliance (e.g. boiler or wood-burning stove) should have a carbon monoxide alarm. It isn't necessary to have a CO alarm if a fireplace is decorative and the chimney has been blocked.

Landlords should install CO alarms according to the manufacturer's instructions, usually at head height and 1–3 metres away from the fuel-burning source.

As with smoke alarms, landlords must carry out a check to ensure that the carbon monoxide alarms are in proper working order when a new tenancy begins. Ensure they are tested and recorded in the Inventory Report at the start of the tenancy.

Tenants should check the alarms once a year. However, I ask the gas engineer to do this when they do the Gas Safety Certificate, and to make a note of it.

Landlords are responsible for repairing or replacing any faulty alarms. Given the low cost, it's easier simply to replace them.

> **TIP**
>
> Buy smoke and carbon monoxide alarms with 10-year batteries and write the installation date on the back of them. Then make a note in your calendar or property management software of when you need to replace them.

Fire safety

Landlords need to assess the risk of fire before letting a property.

Single let houses

Landlords of single let houses can assess the risk themselves if they feel they are competent, but appointing a professional assessor provides greater assurance of compliance. It's best practice to carry out the assessment annually. Landlords may prefer to arrange for a professional to carry it out. Consider providing a fire extinguisher as standard.

Here is a link to the government fire risk assessment checklist.[3]

HMOs

There are higher standards for HMOs. It is advisable for HMO landlords to hire a fire risk assessor and liaise with their local council to ensure they're compliant with the rules. In particular, under the HMO Management Regulations, the HMO manager must keep the means of escape from the HMO free from obstruction and in good repair.

The manager should check this regularly to see (for instance) that there are no hazards in the way, such as bikes blocking the exit. The manager must also keep in good working order fire-fighting equipment such as fire extinguishers and fire blankets, together with fire alarms.

Flats

The rules are more complicated if a landlord is also the

3. GOV.UK, *Fire safety risk assessment: 5-step checklist*, https://www.gov.uk/government/publications/fire-safety-risk-assessment-5-step-checklist.

freeholder of a block of flats, or other building with two or more "sets of domestic places".[4]

Under the Regulatory Reform (Fire Safety) Order 2005, they will need to appoint a "responsible person" to perform certain duties relating to fire safety for the common parts.

The responsible person is likely to be the freeholder, facilities manager or managing agent. As well as the traditional "common parts", the obligations extend to all doors between the domestic premises and common parts (in other words, the doors to individual flats), the doors and windows in external walls and anything attached to the exterior, including balconies.

If a landlord of one or more individual flats is not the responsible person of the building, they should check to see that the fire assessments are in place for the building and common parts. They should also pass on notices from the freeholder to their renters.

Landlords do also need to carry out the usual fire assessments for their own flats (as opposed to the common parts), as with any rental property, and share the assessments with other responsible persons in the block.

Safety of furniture

The Furniture and Furnishings (Fire) (Safety) Regulations 1988 (as amended) require landlords to ensure that most furniture

---

4. Ministry of Housing, Communities and Local Government, *Building Safety Act 2022*. Guidance. (2022), https://www.gov.uk/guidance/the-building-safety-act.

and soft furnishings provided in their rental properties are made from fire-resistant materials.

However, following amendments to the regulations in 2025,[5] certain items intended for babies and small children (such as cots, highchairs and playpens) are no longer covered by these specific regulations.

Landlords are not responsible for checking whether the tenant's furniture complies with the regulations.

Legionella assessments

Legionella is bacteria that can grow in water stored between 20°C and 45°C. Small droplets of water contaminated by Legionella can cause Legionnaires' disease, a potentially fatal form of pneumonia.

Landlords have a legal duty to assess the risk from exposure to Legionella to ensure the safety of their tenants. The assessment doesn't need to be done by a specialist, but it's best practice to keep a written record of the assessment.

According to the Health and Safety Executive (HSE), the risk is low where there are no hot water tanks and cold water is taken directly from the mains with no storage tanks. The risk is also less where the daily water usage is enough to turn over the whole system. The cold water temperature should be below 20°C, and the hot water above 50°C.

FREE LEGIONELLA GUIDE

See the Health and Safety Executive's useful guide:

5. See The Furniture and Furnishings (Fire) (Safety) (Amendment) Regulations 2025, https://www.legislation.gov.uk/uksi/2025/531/made.

Legionella and Landlords' Responsibilities: https://www.hse.gov.uk/legionnaires/legionella-landlords-responsibilities.htm

3. Tenancy obligations

Landlords are required to comply with the following obligations for each tenancy:

Energy Performance Certificate (EPC)

The EPC is an important document.

Obligation to provide an EPC

A landlord or their agent must make available a valid EPC to the tenant by the time they view the property, if not before.

If the property doesn't have a valid EPC when the landlord wishes to let the property, they must commission an EPC before marketing the property and use all reasonable efforts to have one within seven days.

However, an additional 21 days are allowed if the landlord made reasonable efforts to obtain the EPC in the first seven days.

The advertisement or listing must show the energy performance indicator, which is the coloured graph with the numerical score and letter. The landlord must give a full copy of the EPC, including the assessor's recommendation report, to the person who rents the property.

The current minimum energy efficiency standards (MEES)

The MEES for domestic private rented properties is an EPC rating of E, unless the property has a valid exemption.

Section 42 of the Energy Act 2011 defines "domestic private rented properties" as assured tenancies and tenancies regulated by the Rent Act 1977.[6] This means that the MEES rules don't apply to high and low rent tenancies (above £100,000 pa, and below £1,000 pa in London and £250 pa outside London respectively) or tenancies with a resident landlord.

Once a property has been let, a landlord is not currently under an obligation to obtain another EPC when it expires after ten years. A further EPC will only be needed when the landlord next lets (or sells) the property. However, this is under review by the Government.

In any event, it's a good idea to keep the EPC up to date so you keep tabs on the energy efficiency of the building and will have a certificate ready should the tenants decide to move out.

Changes to EPC requirements for landlords

In the *Warm Homes Plan* published in January 2026,[7] the Government confirmed its intention that all domestic private

6. Note that the requirements for Rent Act tenancies are complex and beyond the scope of this book.
7. Department for Energy Security and Net Zero, *Warm Homes Plan*. Policy Paper (2026), https://www.gov.uk/government/publications/warm-homes-plan.

rented properties in England and Wales will need to have either an EPC C from 1 October 2030, or a valid exemption.

Also, the way in which EPCs are measured is due to change from the cost-based Energy Efficiency Rating to the Home Energy Model (HEM) on 1 October 2029.

Under the HEM, a property will need to meet the Fabric Performance Metric, i.e. insulation, window quality and airtightness. The owner will have a choice of either the Heat Performance Metric (e.g. heat pump), the Smart Readiness Metric, or "micro-generation" such as solar powers, smart meters and batteries.

The *Home Energy Model: Energy Performance Certificates* consultation published 21 January 2026 proposed that "no home that relies on a primary fossil-fuel space or water heating system (such as a gas boiler) should be able to achieve a C on the new Heating System Metric".[8]

Properties that achieve an EPC C rating by 1 October 2029 under the Energy Efficiency Rating will be deemed to be compliant until the certificate expires.

Protect tenancy deposit with deposit protection scheme

Section 213 of the Housing Act 2004 makes it compulsory for landlords to protect tenant deposits with a deposit protection scheme within 30 days of receiving the money.

The landlord also must ensure that the tenant receives the

8. Department for Energy Security and Net Zero, *Home Energy Model: Energy Performance Certificates.* Consultation. (2026), https://www.gov.uk/government/consultations/home-energy-model-energy-performance-certificates.

prescribed information concerning the registration of the tenancy deposit, together with a signed deposit protection certificate, within 30 days of handing over the deposit.

Landlords cannot gain possession under all section 8 grounds other than those relating to anti-social behaviour unless the deposit is protected in an authorised scheme and the tenant has been given the prescribed information.

However, unlike with section 21, the court will be able to grant an order for possession under section 8 if these are not done within the 30 days, so long as they are done before the court grants the order.

Although it is possible to delegate this to a letting agent, the landlord remains liable if it is not done. Consequently, landlords should set a calendar reminder to follow up with the agent and check it's done before the 30 days are up.

If the landlord or agent doesn't follow the rules, a tenant can make a claim in court for up to three times the amount of the deposit, plus the return of the original deposit.

Not unlawfully evict or harass a tenant

The Protection from Eviction Act 1977 makes it unlawful for landlords to recover possession of a property from a tenant without a court order or to harass a tenant.

If a landlord serves a possession notice under section 8 HA88 and the tenant doesn't move out voluntarily, the landlord cannot forcibly remove the tenant. Instead, they need to obtain an order for possession from the court.

The RRA introduced the right for local authorities to impose a civil penalty of up to £40,000 as an alternative to prosecution for unlawful eviction or harassment.

ASAF AND FREYA

Asaf has a large portfolio of flats in north Kent that he is looking to sell so he can invest the proceeds into crypto.

Freya rents one of his flats, and Asaf keeps coming round every evening, banging on the door to offer her £1,000 to leave. When she doesn't let him in, he shouts through the letterbox: "Take the cash, or you'll get nothing when I force you out!" This is harassment.

The following week he returns with a locksmith when she is at work, gains entry to the flat and changes the locks. He leaves her belongings by the bins for the flats. This is unlawful eviction.

Not charge prohibited fees

The Tenant Fees Act 2019 prevents landlords or their letting agents from charging tenants and their guarantors most types of fees. See the section on tenant fees in Chapter 9 for full details.

A breach of the Act is a civil offence with a potential fine of up to £5,000. If the landlord commits a further breach within five years of the civil penalty, it will be a criminal offence, which is a banning order offence with an unlimited fine. The local authority may impose a financial penalty of up to £30,000 as an alternative to prosecution. A tenant can claim repayment of any unlawfully charged fees.

Section 9 RRA expanded the Tenant Fees Act to ban inviting, encouraging or accepting rent payments before the tenancy agreement is entered into by both parties.

Private Rented Sector Database

As explained in Chapter 2, once the Database launches, it will be compulsory to have active entries on it for both the landlord and the property before marketing a property for letting. Landlords will be responsible for uploading the relevant safety certificates, although this can be delegated to an agent.

Civil penalties of up to £7,000 will apply for non-compliance with these obligations. This will increase to £40,000 for the offences of providing false information and committing a repeated breach within five years. Landlords will be subject to rent repayment orders for up to two years' rent if they commit these offences.

PRS Landlord Ombudsman

All private landlords will need to join the PRS Landlord Ombudsman before marketing a property to let, even if they use an agent.

The *Implementation Roadmap* estimates that the Ombudsman will be launched in 2028.

Data protection and privacy

Landlords often hold personal information about both their applicants and tenants that could lead to identity theft if the information fell into the wrong hands.

The information that landlords typically hold includes the tenant's name, current and previous addresses, date of birth, place of birth, nationality (as part of the Right to Rent checks), employment details, income, bank details, credit history, etc.

Landlords must hold all information securely and not keep information that they no longer need.

Landlords should have a Data Protection Notice for Tenants which sets out who they are, what information they collect and hold and how they use it.

There are lots of good resources about data protection for landlords on the ICO website.[9]

Register with the ICO

Unless you're the most hands-off landlord and you hold no information on your tenants, you'll need to register with the Information Commissioner's Office (ICO) and pay a fee each year.

The ICO has advised that landlords must pay a fee to register with them if they are doing any of the following activities:[10]

- process personal data for the purpose of producing tenancy agreements/contracts
- perform credit checks via a credit reference agency on prospective tenants
- obtain references

9. Information Commissioner's Office, *Advice for Small and Medium Organisations,* https://ico.org.uk/for-organisations/advice-for-small-organisations.

10. Information Commissioner's Office, *Paying a Data Protection Fee – Real Estate Sector,* https://ico.org.uk/rst.

- keep a database of potential tenants
- make a decision as to which tenant can rent a property, or
- receive electronic copies of tenancy agreements.

It's very easy to register online, and it takes about five minutes.[11] The ICO will email you with a request for payment after you've applied to register. The fee for a landlord to register with the ICO was £52 at the date of publication, although there is a £5 discount if payment is by direct debit.[12]

If you own properties through a limited company, and not in your own name, the ICO registration should be in the name of the limited company.

Comply with the Decent Homes Standard

The Decent Homes Standard (DHS) was originally introduced in 2002 to help improve the quality of housing in the social rented sector. The RRA extends the DHS to the private rented sector, by creating a new DHS that will apply to both social and private rented housing from 2035.

The Government published the *DHS Policy Statement* in January 2026, after carrying out a consultation in 2025.[13] This policy statement confirms the outline of the DHS and the

---

11. Landlords can register and pay the fee using this link on the ICO website: https://ico.org.uk/for-organisations/data-protection-fee/register.
12. GOV.UK, *Pay the Data Protection Fee*, https://www.gov.uk/data-protection-register-notify-ico-personal-data.
13. Ministry of Housing, Communities and Local Government, *The New Decent Homes Standard: Policy Statement* (2026), https://www.gov.uk/government/consultations/consultation-on-a-reformed-decent-homes-standard-for-social-and-privately-rented-homes/outcome/the-new-decent-homes-standard-policy-statement.

implementation date of 2035, with further information to follow.

The *DHS Policy Statement* stated that a property will need to meet the following five criteria to be considered decent:

Criterion A: It must meet the statutory minimum standard.

The property would need to be free of serious hazards (Category 1 hazards) under the Housing Health and Safety Rating System (HHSRS).

This is already a legal requirement, covering risks like severe damp, excess cold and dangerous electrics.

Criterion B: It must be in a reasonable state of repair.

When determining whether a property is in a reasonable state of repair, the focus will be on the condition of the building components, rather than the age.

For "key" building components, a home will fail this criterion if one of more of these needed replacing or major repair. Key components include the roof, chimney, external doors, windows, walls, kitchen, bathroom, electrical system and heating system.

For "other" building components, such as gutters, downpipes, balustrades and handrails, a home will fail the standard if two or more were in a state of disrepair and needed replacing or major repair.

Criterion C: It must have core facilities and services

To pass the DHS, a flat will need to provide at least three of the following core facilities and services:

1. A kitchen with adequate space and layout.
2. An appropriately located bathroom and WC.
3. Adequate external noise insulation.
4. Adequate size and layout of common entrance areas for blocks of flats

Houses will need to provide two of the following core facilities and services:

1. A kitchen with adequate space and layout.
2. An appropriately located bathroom and WC.
3. Adequate external noise insulation.

The *DHS Policy Statement* also confirmed that child-resistant window restrictors will need to be installed on windows that present a fall risk, i.e. those with a sill height below 1100mm.

Criterion D: It must provide a reasonable degree of thermal comfort

The *DHS Policy Statement* confirmed that the home must meet the relevant minimum energy efficiency standard (MEES), which is currently EPC E (although the Government confirmed in the *Warm Homes Plan* that this will increase to EPC C on 1 October 2030).[14]

---

14. DESNZ, *Warm Homes Plan* (2026).

The main heating system also must be capable of heating the whole home, not just a few rooms.

Criterion E: It must be free from damp and mould

This will be a new addition to the Decent Homes Standard, explicitly requiring that properties are "free from damp and mould" beyond the most minor levels.

A home will fail the new DHS if an HHSRS assessment finds any meaningful damp or mould hazard, with only the mildest signs of mould (Bands I or J), which indicate little to no risk to human health, falling outside this criterion.

Also, if the mould is creating a significant risk of harm, landlords will be required to take action within the timescales set out under Awaab's Law, when in force.

We now move on to the final foundational chapter, which is an in-depth guide to choosing, using and managing letting agents in Chapter 4.

CHAPTER 4

USING LETTING AGENTS

Many landlords use letting agents to find tenants and manage the relationship and the property afterwards, as they don't have the time, expertise or inclination to do it themselves, or maybe they're not local to the property.

Good letting agents can make being a landlord easy, but the wrong choice of agent can make life difficult, particularly if they provide a bad service to your tenants.

In this part, I share tips to help landlords choose letting agents, whether it's just to find tenants or for full-blown property management, starting with the law of agency, which underpins the relationship between landlords and letting agents.

1. The law of agency

Unlike most service providers, a letting agent can act in the name of a landlord and make legally binding commitments on behalf of the landlord. They can even enter into agreements with third parties which bind the landlord.

This is because the relationship between a landlord and a letting agent is governed by the law of agency, where a principal authorises an agent to deal with third parties.

When it comes to letting, the landlord is the principal who authorises the letting agent to act on their behalf with tenants and suppliers, including signing the tenancy agreement, receiving rent and serving formal notices. Anything that the agent does for the landlord in the normal course of letting a property is binding on the landlord and is as if the landlord did it themselves.

An agent can bind a landlord, despite not actually being authorised, if it appears to the tenant that the agent has authority to do things on the landlord's behalf. That is called "ostensible" or "apparent" authority.

If an agent signs the tenancy agreement on behalf of a landlord, the agreement is legally binding, even if the landlord specifically told the agent they did not wish to let to that tenant. Another example is where a landlord tells an agent they cannot accept tenants with pets, as it infringes their lease, but the agent signs the tenancy agreement on behalf of the landlord with someone who has a pet. The landlord could bring a claim against the letting agent, but the tenancy agreement would be enforceable by the tenant.

It's the same when an agent manages property: agents' actions bind landlords, so long as it's something that letting agents would ordinarily do.

This is one of the many reasons why landlords need to be very careful when they choose agents and make sure that the agent has very clear written instructions about the scope of their authority and what the landlord needs to authorise.

2. The services letting agents provide

Letting agents offer landlords the following three broad categories of service, at different price points.

Tenant-find service

A tenant-find service (also called let-only) is a basic service where the letting agent finds a suitable tenant on a one-off basis. The fee is usually payable upfront and is around one month's rent plus VAT.

Once the tenant moves in, the letting agent hands over the relationship with the tenant to the landlord, who will manage the property themselves. There's no obligation to use the agent again after the tenant leaves, or if the landlord wishes to increase the rent.

However, landlords must check what's included in the basic let-only fee and what's charged as an extra.

Be aware that many agents in London charge an on-going fee for finding a tenant that is payable for so long as the tenant remains in the property, even if the landlord or another agent manages the property.

Rent collection or rent management

A rent collection service (also called rent management) typically includes a tenant-find service as well as collecting rent from tenants on behalf of the landlord.

This involves chasing up rent arrears, sending regular statements to the landlord and assisting if the tenants don't pay the rent in full. It doesn't include debt collection or providing legal advice, unless the agent has arranged legal insurance for the landlord.

Rent collection doesn't involve management of the property, although it usually includes checking the tenant in and out, organising check-in and check-out inventories (at extra cost) and handling the return of the deposit and any deductions.

Rent collection costs around 8–13% + VAT of the gross rent as an on-going monthly charge. The agent deducts their fee from the rent before sending it on to the landlord.

This is popular with agents in London who offer rent collection to enable them to charge an on-going fee for finding tenants, instead of a one-off payment, which is standard practice outside London.

Full management

With full management, the letting agent takes care of the management of the rental property on the landlord's behalf. It includes tenant-find, rent collection, tenant management and property management, including repairs and property inspections.

The headline fees for full management range from 10–20% plus VAT of the gross rent, but again, it's important to read the small print, as there are often extras like an annual "compliance fee" and charges for rent increases.

As the fees of a tenant-find are usually not much less than one year's full management fees, it can be tempting for landlords to choose full management. However, with a tenant-find, it's usually a one-off fee outside London, whereas with full management, a landlord will need to pay the commission for as long as they use the letting agent. When the rent increases, the fee increases as well.

Some agents also offer a "premium" service which includes rent guarantee insurance. However, it is usually cheaper to obtain rent guarantee insurance direct with the insurance provider yourself.

3. What to look for when choosing agents

Unfortunately, it can be hard to tell if a letting agent is competent and reliable. They might have the right patter, a smart-looking website and appear competent, but just about anyone can set up as a letting agent.

Letting agents currently don't even need a licence or any qualifications.

However, that may change if the recommendations of Lord Best's *Regulation of Property Agents: Working group report*[1] are implemented. This now seems increasingly likely, as the *Home Buying and Selling Reform Consultation* (2025) referred to introducing "a Code of Practice setting out the minimum standards expected of all residential property agents, including estate, letting and managing agents". [2]

The consultation also proposed introducing "mandatory qualifications when a suitable legislative vehicle is available"

---

1. Ministry of Housing, Communities & Local Government, *Regulation of Property Agents: Working Group Report* (2019), https://www.gov.uk/government/publications/regulation-of-property-agents-working-group-report.
2. Ministry of Housing, Communities & Local Government, *Consultation: Home Buying and Selling Reform* (2025), https://www.gov.uk/government/consultations/home-buying-and-selling-reform.

and also that the Government would "consider legislation to ensure compliance with the Code of Practice".

With the absence of minimum professional qualifications and the fact that letting agents can bind landlords legally, landlords need to be very careful when choosing letting agents.

It's easy to go for the big brand name, as they'll have good marketing and vaunt their affiliations. But often it's the smaller, local, independent agent who offers excellent service and continuity of personnel.

Speak to other landlords in your area to see who they do and don't recommend.

Here are some questions to consider when looking for a good agent:

Do they have the right attitude?

As a good landlord, you'll want your property to be well-maintained and your tenants to be treated with respect and courtesy. You need an agent who has a sense of urgency and cares about the experience of your tenants.

Quiz them to check whether they have the right attitude and skills, particularly when it comes to HMOs.

If you're looking for full management, ask them what they think good property management involves. Is the agent focused on providing a smooth, efficient service for the tenant, whilst making sure the property is well-maintained? How do they measure their performance internally? Think about what their choice of metrics says about their approach to customers.

Will they give the right impression to tenants?

The reason you hire letting agents is for them to help you attract and keep good tenants and look after your property for you. They're your representatives.

When thinking about which agents to choose, bear in mind the experience that tenants will have. Will the letting agents give a good impression of you as a landlord? Call the office and see how long they take to answer the phone. How professional are they? Enquire about a property and see what they ask you and how they treat you.

Also review their rental listings on the property portals, as this is what your prospective tenants will see. Are the photos professional? Is there a floor plan and virtual tour? Are the descriptions well written? Does the listing include an EPC? If you wouldn't call up about these properties as a tenant, your future tenants are unlikely to, either.

Is their website clear?

Good letting agents are transparent on their fees and have a clear website. Bearing in mind it's a legal obligation to publish their fees on their website, if their fees aren't easy to find, it means they aren't focused on the needs of their customers and don't walk the talk on being open and transparent.

If everything is clear and easy to find, that's a big tick.

Are they genuinely knowledgeable?

There is no point in hiring letting agents if they're not knowledgeable.

Chat to them to see how well they know the local rental market. Can they give you data about market rents? This will be important when you set and increase the rent, as tenants can challenge the initial rent and subsequent rent increases at the First-tier Tribunal, and the rent will be reduced if the tribunal concludes it is above the market rent for a similar property in the area.

Find out what market segments they specialise in. Do they let lots of properties like yours? If you're an HMO landlord who rents on a per room basis, you want to choose agents that have good expertise in HMOs and are used to dealing with the volume. Likewise, if your target market is families, a letting agent that deals mostly with HMOs might not be right for you.

Are they members of a professional body?

You should check if the agency is a member of a professional body, such as Propertymark[3] or RICS,[4] in addition to a redress scheme.

Membership of a professional organisation signals that an agency has voluntarily subjected itself to strict codes of practice, and independent financial audits, which offers you more protection.

That said, there are many excellent agents who are not members of professional bodies. If they aren't, ask them why they haven't joined. They may have a good reason.

---

3. Propertymark, https://www.propertymark.co.uk.
4. RICS, https://www.rics.org.

Are their staff qualified?

The private rented sector is subject to highly complex legislation, with significant civil penalties for breach of legal obligations, so it is vitally important that the staff managing your day-to-day compliance know exactly what they are doing.

Therefore, you should ask how many of their staff hold at least a Level 3 qualification (roughly equivalent to an A-Level), as this demonstrates that they haven't just picked things up as they went along, but have passed formal exams on the legislation.

The most common qualification is Propertymark's Level 3 Award in Residential Letting & Property Management or their Level 3 Certificate in Property Agency.[5]

However, there are equivalent qualifications from other bodies with Ofqual-regulated benchmarks of competence, such as the Chartered Institute of Housing (CIH)[6] and ABBE.[7]

If you have a particularly large portfolio or complex needs, you might even look for a senior manager with a Level 4 qualification, which is the equivalent to the first year of a university degree.

Be wary of agents who vaguely mention "in-house training" or "attendance certificates". Unlike formal Level 3 qualifications,

---

5. Propertymark qualifications: https://www.propertymark.co.uk/pmq.html.
6. CIH Level 3 Certificate in Letting and Managing Residential Property, more information is available at: https://www.cih.org/housing-academy-qualifications/cih-level-3-certificate-in-letting-and-managing-residential-property.
7. ABBE Level 3 Certificate for Estate and Lettings Agents (CELA), more information is available at: https://www.abbeqa.co.uk/abbe-level-3-certificate-for-estate-and-lettings-agents.

these do not guarantee that the agent has been tested on their knowledge of the law.

Do they understand the Renters' Rights Act?

The Renters' Rights Act has made so many fundamental changes to the relationship between tenants and landlords that it is not enough to know they have a qualification in the law before the Renters' Rights Act.

You need to be confident that they understand the obligations so that they will not expose you to the significant civil penalties for breaches of the obligations, not least because landlords can be held liable for the actions of agents acting on their behalf.

Ask what training their staff have had, and how they have changed their processes; for instance, their approach to stating the specific proposed rent in all written adverts and not inviting or accepting offers above this.

Quiz them on their tenant screening process. Do they apply blanket bans on families with children or applicants receiving benefits? If your agent automatically filters out these applicants, you could be liable for rental discrimination. Ask to see their screening criteria to ensure they assess every applicant on their individual merits.

How do they handle common problems?

If using agents for full management, ask how tenants log repairs. How long does it take on average for repairs to be completed after the tenant reports the issue? Do they even measure this? How would they respond to a tenant who reports a broken boiler on the Friday evening of a Bank Holiday weekend? Would they get a gas engineer out straight away, or wait until Tuesday or Wednesday?

Ask how they approach reports of damp and mould. An agent who immediately says it's always the tenant's fault does not understand how and why damp and mould arise and may not manage this common issue properly.

If they explain it's important to find the source of the damp, then they're on the right lines. Often there is more than one reason for damp and mould, and they need to appreciate that it's not always the tenant's "lifestyle" that causes mould.

How often do they carry out inspections?

Ask how often they inspect the property as standard. Some agents only include one inspection every 12 months, which is not enough. Inspections should be carried out at least every 6 months to check the property in summer and winter and to keep an eye on the condition of the property.

Not only do many insurance companies require regular inspections, but a lot can go wrong in 12 months.

Who will you be dealing with on a day-to-day basis?

Letting agents will usually have separate departments for lettings and property management. Therefore, it's unlikely that the person who found the tenants will manage the property for you. Some agents manage properties locally, and others have a dedicated team in the region or even nationally.

Ask what level of customer care you will receive. Will you have a named person as a relationship manager, or is it just a centralised number? What form of reporting do they provide you with as a customer? Do they offer a yearly review? As mentioned above, what qualifications do they have?

4. Using agents to find tenants

For landlords who wish to benefit from professional marketing and vetting of applicants, but want to carry out the management themselves, a tenant-find service offers a practical middle ground. This section explores what to expect from a tenant-find service, how much it's likely to cost and tips for using letting agents to find tenants for you.

How much does a tenant-find service cost?

The basic tenant find fee

The basic "tenant-find" or "tenant introduction" fee is often around one month's rent plus VAT. Some agents will charge a flat fee instead of an amount that is linked to the rent.

Be aware that in London, agents may ask for an on-going fee that will remain payable for so long as the tenant stays in the property.

The basic fee for a tenant find usually includes:

- carrying out basic compliance checks.
- advising what the proposed rent should be.
- listing the property compliantly on the property portals.

- arranging and carrying out the viewings, and giving feedback on the viewings.
- receiving offers.
- preparing a short list of applicants.
- negotiating the rent (which cannot be higher than the proposed rent).
- receiving the first month's rent.

What extras should landlords look out for

Some letting agents charge extra for services that other agents include in the basic fee. It's therefore so important to understand what's included and what's excluded, looking at the total cost and not the headline fee.

It is a legal requirement under section 82 of the Consumer Rights Act 2015 for letting agents to publish their fees for letting and property management services on their websites, as well as in their premises. The description of the fee needs to be sufficiently detailed so that the landlord understands how much the agent will charge for a given service.

Check the small print carefully, as an agent with a low basic fee might charge extra for services which other agents include in the basic fee.

Here are examples of additional fees that agents often charge on top of the basic tenant find fee:

Tenancy agreement preparation

Most agents will charge extra for preparing the tenancy agreement, even though it'll be their standard template. The charge will usually include electronic signing.

The charges range from around £200 to £450 including VAT in 2026.

Tenancy deposit registration fee

Most agents charge an administration fee to handle the deposit registration process on your behalf.

This cost usually varies from £30 to £85, although some agents charge landlords an annual deposit compliance fee. (See Chapter 9 for more details.)

Compliance fees

Some agents charge extra to check smoke alarms, carbon monoxide alarms and safety certification at the start of a tenancy. This can be a one-off fee or a monthly fee for landlords who have full management, or an upfront fee for landlords who use a tenant-find-only service.

These fees are controversial, as the inventory clerk will check the smoke and carbon monoxide alarms, and the rest of the compliance should be included, not least because the letting agents cross-sell other services such as EPCs and Gas Safety Certificates.

Check-in inventory

Letting agents usually subcontract the preparation of inventories to companies who specialise in inventories.

The price of an inventory increases in line with the number of bedrooms and starts from around £150 for an unfurnished three-bedroomed house. Inventories are more expensive for furnished properties than unfurnished properties. It can be cheaper to go direct to inventory clerks.

Tenant referencing and Right to Rent checks

Agents charge from around £50 to carry out referencing and Right to Rent checks on each adult tenant.

Other extra services and costs

It's important to read the fee schedule to make sure there won't be any surprises at a later date. Here are a few extras to look out for when using agents on a tenant-find basis:

- Is professional photography included as standard? If so, is there an additional fee?
- Will the agent prepare a floor plan? If so, is there an additional fee?
- Are there any additional fees payable in the future?
- Ask what the total charges are for the tenancy deposit protection, i.e. the initial charge, any annual charge, assistance in the event of a dispute, or the transfer of the deposit to a custodial account in the name of the landlord.
- Is there a separate "compliance check" or "safe and legal check"? Ask for a list of precisely what checks it covers. As the inventory clerk will test smoke and carbon monoxide alarms as part of the inventory, it's unreasonable for agents to charge for a check that the landlord has already paid for.
- Do they insist on a formal Legionella risk assessment by a third-party contractor? This will rarely be necessary, unless it's a licensing requirement.

- What are the arrangements for the inventory? Is it just a flat fee according to the number or bedrooms, or do they charge an administration fee on top? Do they charge the check-out fee in advance?

Tips for using letting agents to find tenants

My experience is that landlords need to manage letting agents and make clear their expectations when engaging them to find tenants.

Here are six tips for using letting agents to find tenants:

1. Don't be afraid to negotiate

The lettings industry is highly competitive, and agents are always looking for new landlords.

There will usually be some room for negotiation over fees and terms, and it's always easier to negotiate as a potential client than if you've already been using them. Landlords with a portfolio can often negotiate a discount. If you don't ask, you don't get.

That said, the cheapest isn't necessarily the best, and it's important to understand what service level you will get in return.

2. Be clear about your selection criteria for tenants

Letting agents aren't telepathic. Let them know your selection criteria in advance but do remember that the RRA has outlawed bans on families and applicants on benefits (in addition to the existing law on discrimination which I explain in Chapter 8).

However, you can make clear the maximum number of people you want living in the property, and whether you'll accept sharers from different households or prefer one household.

Clearly, if there are three or more sharers from different households, it will be an HMO, so you'll need to know whether the local council has introduced additional licensing for your postcode.

3. Check the description and the floor plan

Ask to check the description and the floor plan before the property is listed on the portals to make sure it's accurate. When I used agents for tenant-finds, I spotted at least one mistake in every advertisement, including the floor plan.

Having an accurate description means that tenants will have a good idea of what the property is like, before making the effort to attend a viewing. Ensuring that the description of your property is accurate is part of being professional.

4. Let them know if you're going to be carrying out any work

If you plan to do some work on the property before the tenants move in, it's a good idea to email the agent with a pdf document that explains what will be done so that the person who does the viewings can tell applicants.

This saves the applicants asking if something is going to be repaired, because they will already know. It also helps the agent if you provide accurate information in writing.

5. Tell the agents if you want to meet the shortlist

Unless you want absolutely nothing to do with your tenants and prefer having the relationship entirely managed by the agents, it's a good idea to meet the preferred candidates, if not the shortlist, before authorising the agent to proceed with the tenancy agreement.

Tenant selection is even more important now as the RRA has changed the nature of the relationship between landlords and tenants into a longer-term relationship. Landlords can no longer serve a "no fault" section 21 eviction notice if it's not working out. Instead, landlords can only terminate a tenancy for one of the reasons specified in section 8.

It's therefore safer to be comfortable that the letting agent has made the right choice by meeting the applicants first.

6. Ask to see the reference report

Letting agents will outsource referencing to specialist providers who provide them with a report. Ask to see the report, and they can't refuse if you are registered with the ICO and have a Data Protection Notice.[8]

After all, under the law of agency, they are acting on your behalf, and you are their principal.

5. Using agents for full property management

Self-managing a rental property isn't for everyone. There may

8. See the section on Data Protection in Chapter 3.

be many reasons why it would be better for you to use an agent to manage your property and your tenants. For instance, if you don't live within easy reach of the property, don't have the time or inclination or prefer to keep a professional distance between you and your tenants.

However, as with using agents for finding tenants, the cost and service levels vary considerably with full property management.

In this section, I focus on the costs involved in paying agents for full property management. I cover how to use letting agents effectively for property management in Chapter 11.

How much does full management cost?

As mentioned above, letting agents have a legal duty to publish their fees for property management services on their website, as well as in their premises.

The fully managed service is a bit like full board at a hotel. Your food and lodging are included, but you may need to pay for drinks and a number of extras. It's not all-inclusive, and the exact detail of what you get varies from agent to agent.

In order to avoid problems later on, and maybe even negotiate a better deal with your agent upfront, it's important to check what is and isn't included in the basic property management fee.

The basic property management fee

Most agents charge landlords a basic fee to provide a full management service that is usually a percentage of the rent. Fees for full management range from around 10% plus VAT

(12%) to 17% plus VAT (20.4%) of the gross rent per calendar month.

The fee for full property management will usually include the following services:

- Finding tenants, as discussed above, although some agents charge an additional set-up fee. This is technically a separate service, but it's commonly bundled with property management.
- Meter readings and the changeover of utilities at the start and end of a tenancy (agents sometimes have preferred suppliers who give them commission).
- Acting as a point of contact for tenants, providing a professional distance for the landlord during the tenancy.
- Arranging repairs and maintenance for the landlord up to a certain pre-approved amount.
- Holding keys for the property.
- One inspection each year, but some carry out inspections every six months.
- Collecting rent and sending it on to the landlord. Chasing "initial arrears" from tenants (not formal debt collection).
- Checking safety certificates and arranging renewals e.g. Gas Safety Certificate (charged separately). Some agents charge a separate compliance fee for this.
- Uploading documents onto the PRS Database, when it is launched.
- Managing rent increases, i.e. completion and service of a section 13 notice, and subsequent negotiation.
- Managing the check-out of the tenant, organising a

final inventory (at extra cost) and handling the return of the deposit and any deductions.

Landlords pay the fee even if nothing goes wrong with the property, and even if the rent is in arrears, for so long as these tenants rent the property, unless the landlord terminates the management contract.

The agents deduct the fee from the monthly rent which they collect on the landlord's behalf. If the rent goes up, the fee goes up in parallel, as it's a form of commission.

Don't be afraid to negotiate lower rates before you sign up. It's usually easier to do it then, as they're keen to win your business. Just like negotiating car insurance!

However, the cheapest agent isn't always the best. You should look for value for money. This means a good level of service for you and your tenants, which leaves the agent with a fair profit.

What extras should landlords look out for?

It's a good idea to print out the list of fees and go through them carefully to make sure there is nothing unexpected.

Here are a few charges to watch out for:

Repairs and maintenance

Agents will usually manage repairs and maintenance for the landlord. However, many charge a mark-up of 10% or more on the invoices. Check what this is for. Do they actually supervise the works in person or are they just acting as a glorified call centre? Do you have the right to use your own contractors?

Check when the landlord needs to approve work – usually there's a monetary amount, e.g. over £250 plus VAT.

Compliance fees

As we saw in the section on tenant-finds, some of the larger agents charge an additional "compliance" fee on top of the basic management fee and link their liability under the agreement to payment of this fee.

Compliance should come as part of the basic fee for property management, so it is worth negotiating for the compliance fee to be removed.

Refuse to accept any clause that says the agent's liability to indemnify the landlord is subject to the landlord's payment of the compliance *fee.*

"Renewal" fees

Before the RRA outlawed fixed-term tenancies, it was common for agents to arrange for tenants to "renew" each time it expired, by issuing a new tenancy agreement for the parties to sign, often with a higher rent. This was an easy way for letting agents to earn additional fees.

Now that the RRA has made all tenancies periodic, it is no longer possible to "renew" a tenancy. However, while agents can legitimately charge for renegotiating the rent and dealing with the section 13 procedure, do watch out for terms that require the landlord to pay another fee on the anniversary of the start of a tenancy.

Is there a unilateral right to increase fees?

Check to see whether the agent has the right to increase the fees or impose new fees without the agreement of the landlord.

Unless the landlord also has the right to terminate the agreement after an increase in the fees, this will be an unfair term for consumer landlords under the Consumer Rights Act 2015.

It's worth bearing in mind that an increase in fees can be an easy way to terminate an agreement with a letting agent.

What is a "consumer landlord"?

As mentioned above, a landlord has some protection against unfair terms in contracts if they are acting as a "consumer".

A landlord is a consumer if they are an individual who is "acting for purposes that are wholly or mainly outside that individual's trade, business, craft or profession".

CONSUMER LANDLORDS

Full-time doctor. They are likely to be a consumer when dealing with letting agents as they are not acting in their profession as a doctor. It doesn't matter how many properties they have. They could have ten rental properties and be an experienced landlord, but if they have another job, they're likely to benefit from consumer protection laws.

Limited companies. Landlords who own rental properties through limited companies are not consumers and they have no protection from unfair terms in contracts with letting agents. This is because only "individuals" (i.e. human beings) can be consumers.

6. The terms of business

Letting agents are notorious for including one-sided terms in their terms of business, so it is vital that landlords read the terms and conditions with agents before signing up.

AI models such as Claude, ChatGPT and Gemini can be really useful in helping you uncover what's buried in the small print.

Don't let the agent rush you into signing up. Taking another day to get the property listed won't matter. Ask the agent to send you the draft agency agreement with all the fees included in advance, so you have no surprises. Don't be afraid to negotiate.

If something seems unreasonable, you can go elsewhere. There are many letting agents and you shouldn't feel pressured into signing up with an agency that overcharges or has unreasonable terms.

And do read the small print before you sign off. Make sure that the agents confirm in writing any agreement you reach with them that differs from their standard terms.

Here are a few tips on what to look out for:

Termination provisions

The very first clause you should check is the termination clause. Things change, and you may wish to take over management in the future or move to another agent. This is your right.

Check whether you can give a reasonable amount of notice to terminate, for instance, two months' notice after the first year? Or do the terms and conditions include a penalty (say two months' gross rent), sometimes called a "withdrawal fee", which effectively ties the landlord in until the tenant moves out?

As I explained above, agents in London often charge for the tenant-find for as long as the tenant remains in the property, even if they are no longer managing the property.

Even if these types of provisions may be seen as unfair contract terms under consumer protection law for landlords who are consumers (see above), it is far better to have it removed at the start, when the agent is probably more willing to negotiate.

How long are you tied in for?

Sometimes agents don't find tenants quickly, and you might want to move to another.

However, agents will usually tie landlords into a minimum exclusivity period ranging from 8 to 20 weeks, during which time you cannot leave the agent without paying a "withdrawal fee", even if you had no or very few viewings in that period. Also, you may need to give 14 to 28 days' notice to terminate the sole agency.

A letting agent should be able to find a suitable tenant within 8 weeks if the rent is pitched at an appropriate level and they market the property well.

Refuse to accept more than 8 weeks' sole agency and ask for the notice period to be 7 to 14 days.

Unilateral right to increase fees

As mentioned above, check to see if they have the right to increase fees without you having the ability to terminate if you're not happy with the fees.

Commission on a sale

You should look out for a clause that obliges you to pay commission of (say) 1.5% plus VAT of the purchase price if the tenant or someone who the tenant introduces buys the property during or within six months of the end of a tenancy.

Not only is this a high commission, but it means the letting agent is being paid twice for their service. It would be a windfall for the agent.

The High Court case of *The Office of Fair Trading v Foxtons* (2009)[9] held these clauses to be unfair.

7. Terminating a property management contract

Landlords may wish to terminate a property management agreement (or a rent collection service) with an agent for a variety of reasons.

For instance, their personal circumstances may change, and they wish to take over the management themselves.

9. *Office of Fair Trading v Foxtons Ltd* [2009] EWHC 1681 (Ch).

Alternatively, they may wish to move their business to another agent. Or perhaps they wish to terminate because they're unhappy with the service the agents have been providing.

The easiest approach is usually to wait until the tenants move out and terminate the agreement then. However, if you don't wish to wait until they move out, you will need to check the agency agreement to see what the termination provisions state, and whether there is a termination fee.

Termination by notice

Some letting agents have a simple termination clause that will enable you to terminate full management or rent collection by the service of reasonable notice, for instance one or three months.

If the notice period is fair and reasonable (up to three months), then you can serve a notice to terminate, in a similar way to a tenant serving a notice to quit.

If the notice is excessively long, for instance six months after an initial period of a year, landlords who are "consumers" can challenge it as an unfair term.

Unfair termination fees and terms

Unfortunately, some agents make it difficult for landlords to terminate property management contracts, by including a clause in the contract which imposes a high "withdrawal fee", a "termination fee" or an excessively long notice period for the landlord to terminate the agreement.

For instance, a termination fee of two months' rent plus VAT or requiring a notice period of six months or more if the tenant is still there (once an initial period of, say, 12 months has passed).

However, even if you have signed a draconian termination fee that acts as a penalty to stop landlords from terminating, it may not be binding on you if the term is "unfair" and you are a consumer. This is because section 62 of the Consumer Rights Act 2015 states that unfair terms in contracts with consumers are not binding on consumers.

Consequently, if a termination clause is unfair, if you are a landlord who is also a consumer, you can disregard it and refuse to pay it. However, not all landlords are consumers.

Can landlords avoid paying high termination fees?

If there is a high termination fee and you are a consumer, you can write to the agent and say the termination provisions are unfair and, as you're a consumer, it is not binding on you, referring to section 62 of the Consumer Rights Act 2015.

If the agent doesn't back down, and deducts the fee from the final rent payment and/or sends a letter before action threatening a claim in the small claims court, you should write again to the manager of the office, repeat the reasons the clause is not binding and ask to make a complaint under their complaints policy.

Should the outcome of the complaint be unsatisfactory, you can appeal to the agent's redress scheme. Before doing this, take independent legal advice to check that you are a consumer.

Where you can show that the agent has provided a poor service, for instance, failing to carry out inspections or renew the Gas Safety Certificate without good reason, the landlord may be able to terminate without paying a termination fee, citing the agent's fundamental breach of contract.

Again, take independent legal advice to check that the evidence of the poor service is sufficiently robust and that the agent did not carry out the services with reasonable care and skill.

That brings us to the end of Part I: Foundations. We now move on to Part II: Before the tenancy, to discuss what landlords need to do before the tenancy starts.

PART II

BEFORE THE TENANCY

CHAPTER 5

GETTING READY TO LET

Letting a property is heavily regulated, and it's important to take the time to make sure you get the details right, even if you use agents. This chapter guides you through the key steps you need to follow to ensure your property is legally compliant, safe and ready to let to tenants.

1. Licensing

The first important task is to find out whether your property needs a licence from your local authority, as it's a criminal offence under the Housing Act 2004 to "control or manage" a property without a required licence.[1]

If you do need a licence, make sure you apply for the licence before letting the property.

Note that licensing will be separate and in addition to registering on the PRS Database, once it is fully launched.

Different types of licence

There are three different types of licence for landlords:

1. Under s.263 HA 2004, the "person having control" is the person who receives the "rack rent", which is at least two-thirds of the annual rent. This is usually the owner. The "person managing" is the person who receives the rent from the tenants. This could be the owner or the letting agent.

Mandatory licence for HMOs

Under section 254 Housing Act 2004, large Houses in Multiple Occupation (HMOs), with five or more sharers from more than one household, must have a "mandatory licence".

This rule is the same throughout England, although the conditions in mandatory licences do vary from council to council.

Additional licence for HMOs

The 2004 Act also gives local authorities the ability to extend HMO licensing to smaller HMOs with three or more sharers. Licences for these smaller HMOs are called "additional licences".

Some councils use additional licensing to regulate section 257 Housing Act 2004 HMOs, which are converted blocks of flats with self-contained flats which have not met certain building standards and where at least one third of the flats are privately rented.

Selective licence

Councils also have the power to introduce "selective licences" for all rental properties that do not have either a mandatory HMO licence or an additional licence. In areas with selective licensing, all rental properties that aren't already licensed need to have a selective licence.

As the powers to introduce licensing schemes have been devolved to the local authority, the approach differs from local authority to local authority, and even from street to street within a local authority.

How to find out if a property needs a licence

Local authorities regularly introduce new licensing schemes, so even if you don't have a large HMO that is subject to mandatory licensing, you still need to make sure that you're not required to obtain a licence.

Landlords should check this themselves, even if they use agents, as sometimes agents don't inform landlords when councils introduce new licensing schemes.

Unfortunately, there's not a single website to look up the licensing requirements for a property by the postcode across England, as licensing is decentralised and managed by local authorities. This means you'll need to check the website of the appropriate local authority.[2] However, you can look up the licensing requirements for the London boroughs on the website London Property Licensing.[3]

> **TIP**
>
> Local authorities regularly introduce new licensing schemes, so it's important to check whether the property needs a licence at least once a year.

Applying for a licence

The application processes for licensing vary between local

---

2. If you're unsure of the local authority, you can check here: *Find Your Local Counci,l* https://www.gov.uk/find-local-council.
3. London Property Licensing, https://londonpropertylicensing.co.uk.

authorities. While most have adopted an online process, some still rely on paper-based forms. Therefore, you should check the local council's website to find out the exact process.

Licences are usually for five years, and councils provide discounts if the landlord is accredited by one of the accreditation bodies.

Sanctions

Not only is it a criminal offence to let a licensable property without a licence, but prosecution may result in an unlimited fine and a banning order for the landlord. The council may also impose a civil penalty of up to £40,000 as an alternative to prosecution if they are satisfied, beyond reasonable doubt, that the landlord has committed the offence of failing to obtain a licence.

Further, landlords who let licensable properties without a licence could also be subject to a Rent Repayment Order and be required to repay up to 24 months' rental income to the tenants.

2. Consents to let

Depending on the circumstances, you may need to obtain consents from other organisations before letting a property.

For instance, if you're an accidental landlord with a standard residential mortgage, you will need to get either consent to let or re-mortgage using a buy-to-let mortgage if your mortgage company won't grant consent to let.

Landlords who are leaseholders of their property, as opposed to a freeholder, may need to obtain consent to let from their freeholder or their managing agent. Usually this is a formality, although the leaseholder will typically need to pay a standard fee. Do also check whether your lease requires the freeholder's consent for a tenant to keep a pet, as that will be relevant if your tenant wishes to have a pet.

3. Furnished versus unfurnished

According to research published by HMRC in 2025,[4] 72% of the landlords surveyed let properties unfurnished.

Whether it is right for you to let furnished or unfurnished will depend on the expectations of your target tenants, the norms for your area and your own preferences.

If your property is in a city centre, you're likely to have high demand from younger renters and students, and they tend to prefer fully furnished properties.

Corporate lets are usually fully furnished with kitchen appliances, including kettles and toasters, and soft furnishings included. Families tend to prefer unfurnished properties.

If you're not sure of the norm for your area and target tenants, it's a good idea to speak to letting agents. You can also take a look on the property portals to get a feel for what's usual in your area.

Practicalities

In terms of practicalities, it's easier and cheaper not to furnish a rental property. Usually, any additional rent is negligible, and

4. *HMRC Research Report no.804: Landlords Research Findings*, (10 May 2025), p. 11, https://www.gov.uk/government/publications/landlords-research.

you have the on-going cost of replacing items as they wear out. You might also go to the expense of furnishing it, only to be asked to remove some or all of it.

Furnished properties are more high maintenance when it comes to management, as there's more to go wrong. As we saw in Chapter 3, you'll need to organise portable appliance testing (PAT testing) each year for any electrical items. Additionally, any furniture and furnishings need to comply with the Furniture and Furnishings (Fire Safety) Regulations 1988.

Finally, you'll have the added cost of contents insurance, on top of the usual landlord buildings insurance.

Compulsory items

It is compulsory for landlords to provide the following items in all properties, regardless of whether they are furnished or unfurnished:

Light fittings

Light fittings must be safe.

Flooring

Any flooring provided must be safe. Exposed floorboards are acceptable, so long as they are safe to walk on. Leaving underlay and grippers for the tenants to put carpet on top of is not acceptable.

Secure doors

The external doors and doors onto common parts need to be secure, with locks that work properly. It is good practice to change the locks in between tenants, and you should change the locks when you buy a rental property.

Appliances

Appliances are expensive items and are prone to breakages. The more the landlord provides, the more costs you will have when they inevitably break.

For furnished properties, the landlord should supply the basic large appliances such as a hob, stove, fridge and washing machine, although there's no hard and fast rule (unless it's stipulated in a licence, for instance a mandatory licence for an HMO).

If a property is let on an unfurnished basis, the landlord is not obliged to supply any appliances, although most supply a cooker. When determining whether a property is fit for human habitation under section 10 Landlord and Tenant Act, "regard shall be had" to the condition of the "facilities for preparation and cooking of food". This falls short of requiring a landlord to supply these appliances.

Note that the *DHS Policy Statement* refers to "cooker space" in its list of core facilities and services, and not a cooker.[5]

However, if the kitchen has space for integrated appliances,

5. Ministry of Housing, Communities and Local Government, *DHS Policy Statement* (2026).

these should be supplied by the landlord. A tenant does not usually buy integrated appliances for a fitted kitchen.

Many landlords provide a freestanding (or integrated) fridge freezer, although it isn't compulsory. However, it's a fairly low risk / high reward option to provide, although I would avoid one that chills water or has an ice-maker. I also choose one with a long guarantee, just in case.

It's standard for landlords to provide plumbing for washing machines and, increasingly, dishwashers. If you provide freestanding appliances and other "portable" electrical items, it is important to arrange or carry out regular safety PAT testing.

Curtains and blinds

Landlords are not legally required to provide curtains or blinds for tenants. However, it's common practice for landlords to provide curtain poles, curtain rails or blinds for the bedrooms and main front room.

As well as being convenient for tenants, it's wise to provide at least curtain poles or curtain rails, as it prevents tenants from drilling holes to do it themselves, which could lead to wall damage, especially if the house is old.

Take care with blinds, as they need to comply with safety standards.[6]

---

6. See British Blind and Shutter Association, *Advice for Landlords on Window Blind Safety,* (2021), https://www.makeitsafe.org.uk/wp-content/uploads/2021/04/BBSA-Guidance-for-Landlords-v1-April-21.pdf.

4. Preparing the property for tenants

Unless you have a new build property, it's likely that you'll need to do some work to make sure it's in good shape for letting to tenants. Not only will you get a higher rent if the property is clean and in good condition, but you'll also start on a good footing with the tenants. The inventory will show everything is clean and in good repair, which makes it easier to make a claim on the tenancy deposit if the property is not in the same condition at the end of the tenancy.

Whether you're re-letting the property after a tenant has moved out or it's a new purchase, it's important to walk around it with a critical eye to see what needs doing. After all, it's a lot easier to sort out problems when the property is empty than after tenants have moved in.

Here is a checklist with tips of things to look out for when preparing a property for tenants to make sure it is in good repair and properly clean.

Exterior and security

- Do the front and back door keys work properly? It's good practice to arrange for a locksmith to change the locks.
- Do all the windows open and shut properly? Do you have all the window keys?
- What's the state of the guttering and down pipes? Are there signs of water getting in the house? If so, get it repaired.
- Does the garden need any work? Now is a good time to prune any overgrown shrubs, mow the lawn and

sow some grass seed in bare patches, after raking the ground and watering it in. Depending on the season, you might need to water the newly seeded grass for a couple of weeks until it's established.

- Check the patio and paths for any trip hazards.

Interior repair, decoration and cleanliness

- Are the carpets in good condition? I have a carpet cleaner that I use to freshen up carpets between tenants. I also buy good quality, hard-wearing carpet so it only needs replacing every ten years or so.
- Are there any dripping taps, broken light fittings, leaking radiators, plug sockets that don't work?
- If it's light wear and tear, go around with a tin of paint and paint brush to cover up any marks on the walls. Otherwise, consider getting it repainted professionally
- Does the bathroom need new silicone around the bath, shower and basin?
- Does the kitchen need new silicone around the sink and where the tiling meets the work surface?
- Fill in any holes in the walls and repaint.
- Make sure the property is clean throughout to a professional standard, and don't forget to clear the shower trap in the plughole, descale shower heads and clean the filters of the kitchen extractor fan,

Safety and mould prevention

- Are there restrictors on all windows which present a fall risk for children?

- Do the blinds comply with safety standards?
- Are any handrails and balustrades secure?
- Do the extractor fans work in the bathroom and kitchen? (If you don't have vented extractor fans, do put them in, as it'll help reduce condensation.)
- Arrange PAT testing.
- Check the hot water temperature is set to over 50°C and flush the cold water through the system to reduce the risk of Legionella. If there's a hot water tank, check that it's set to store water at 60°C and is well-insulated.

5. Protect your property from fraud

Before you let a property, it's important to protect yourself from property fraud. This includes someone impersonating you to transfer the ownership of the property to someone else or take out a fraudulent mortgage on the property without your knowledge. Most buy-to-let properties have a mortgage, and the lender will have registered the usual restriction against dealing without their consent, but it's best to check to see if you are using all of the available tools.

There are three simple ways to protect your property from fraud:

a. Check the address of the registered proprietor

Make sure that the address of the registered proprietor in the Proprietor Register of the Register of Title has your home address, or the registered office if the owner is a limited company. If it's not, it's easy to change it by completing and returning Form COG1 to HM Land Registry.[7]

Do also keep the address up to date if you move house. It's free to do this, and you don't need to use a solicitor to submit the form.

b. Set up a property alert with HM Land Registry

You can sign up with the Property Alert Service online to receive email alerts when official searches and applications are received against up to ten monitored properties. This service is also free.[8]

c. Put a restriction on your title

You can register a restriction on your title with HM Land Registry to stop HM Land Registry registering a sale or mortgage on your property unless a conveyancer or solicitor certifies you made the application.[9]

You do this yourself by filing Form RQ if you bought the property in your own name, and Form RQ (Co) if a limited company owns the property. [10]

---

7. HM Land Registry, *Form: Update Registered Owners' Contact Address (COG1)*, https://www.gov.uk/government/publications/updating-registered-owners-contact-address.
8. See HM Land Registry, *Property Alert Service*, https://propertyalert.landregistry.gov.uk.
9. See *Protect your Land and Property from Fraud*, https://www.gov.uk/protect-land-property-from-fraud.
10. See *Form: Restriction by Owner Not Living at Property Request: Registration (RQ)*, https://www.gov.uk/government/publications/restriction-by-owner-not-living-at-property-request-registration-rq and *Form: Restriction by Company Request: Registration (RQ(Co))*, https://www.gov.uk/government/publications/restriction-by-company-request-registration-rqco.

Be aware that you'll need to have a solicitor or conveyancer apply to remove the restriction, which might cause a delay when you sell or re-mortgage the property. As mentioned above, if you have a mortgage, there may already be a restriction against dealing.

6. Summary of preparing for let

Here is a consolidated summary of preparing for let, which includes the relevant landlord responsibilities from Part 3:

- Check if the property needs a licence and apply for one if it does.
- Decide if you will let the property on a furnished or unfurnished basis. In any event, make sure there are adequate cooking facilities (a hob and an oven).
- Ensure you have up-to-date safety certificates: a Gas Safety Certificate (within the last twelve months), an EICR (within the last five years), and an EPC (within the last ten years). Obtain new certificates as necessary before letting the property.
- Make sure the property is in a good state of repair and decoration, and clean to a professional standard, using the checklist in Section 4 on how to prepare the property.
- Carry out a fire risk assessment, and check whether the fire extinguisher is in date.
- Carry out a Legionella risk assessment.
- Test portable appliances (PAT testing).
- Check the smoke and carbon monoxide alarms work, and that the batteries don't need replacing.
- Update the property manual with instruction booklets for new appliances.

- Protect your property from fraud by setting up an alert with HM Land Registry and making sure the address of the registered proprietor is not the address of the property.
- Make sure the entry for the property on the PRS Landlord Database is up to date, and upload the requisite documentation, once the Database has launched (likely to be in 2027).

Now we have prepared for letting, we can move on to setting and collecting the initial rent in Chapter 6.

CHAPTER 6

SETTING AND COLLECTING THE INITIAL RENT

In this chapter, I go through what to consider when setting and collecting the rent for new tenants, including the ban on rental bidding, and the complicated rules on advance rent payments in the Renters' Rights Act for assured periodic tenancies.

The rules relating to rent during a tenancy are in Chapter 14.

1. Setting the proposed rent

Setting the rent at the right level is very important. If it's too high, you'll get little interest from prospective tenants. If it's too low, you won't be able to negotiate a higher rent if it's an assured periodic tenancy.

If you use letting agents, they'll be able to advise you what the going rate is for similar properties in your area.

You can also do your own market research by setting up alerts on the property portals for the areas where your buy-to-lets are located. Look at them regularly and see how long it takes for properties to have a "Let Agreed" label. Even when there is high demand, some properties will show as reduced as the rent has been pitched too high.

You can add a Google extension to Chrome that will show you the price change history on Rightmove.

Once you have a feel for which way the market is moving, be objective about the pros and cons of your property compared to the other properties you've seen on the portals. Is the condition of your property better or worse? How is it decorated? Is it bigger or smaller than normal? Does it have a cellar or a loft? What about the location? Is your property on a busy road? How energy efficient is it?

2. The rent period

When you set the rent for an assured periodic tenancy, the period for which the rent is payable (the rent period) must not be longer than one calendar month. Any term in an APT is null and void if it provides for longer rent periods, such as quarterly or six-monthly.

If a pre-RRA assured shorthold tenancy agreement has rent periods of longer than one month, the rent is due monthly on a pro-rata basis, using the formula in the new section 4A(6) HA88.[1]

3. Obligation to specify the proposed rent

When landlords or letting agents are looking for new tenants for an APT, they have a legal obligation under section 56 RRA to specify the proposed rent in any advertisement, listing or offer.

This includes an advertisement or listing on one of the property portals such as Rightmove or Zoopla, on Facebook,

1. The formula in section 4A(6) HA88 pro-rates the rent by dividing the rent due for the first rent period of the tenancy by the number of whole days in that period and multiplying it by 30.42.

Instagram or Gumtree, a website, a printed advert or even a text message or email.

However, "for let" boards outside of a property do not need to state the proposed rent. If a landlord finds a tenant through word of mouth, they must confirm the proposed rent in writing.

The proposed rent must be for a specific amount, and not a range, for a period of no longer than one calendar month.

Once a landlord specifies the proposed rent, they cannot increase it, but they can reduce it if the tenant wishes to put in an offer to pay lower rent.

If a landlord breaches this obligation, the local authority has a duty to enforce it and can impose a civil penalty of up to £7,000 if they are "satisfied on a balance of probabilities" there has been a breach of this obligation. However, the starting point for the penalty in the statutory guidance is £3,000.[2]

4. Ban on rental bidding

Once the proposed rent is published, it acts as a cap, and section 56 RRA bans landlords or anyone acting on their behalf from going above the proposed rent, which is called "rental bidding".

The ban on rental bidding includes the following:

- Asking for offers above the proposed rent.
- Encouraging someone to offer more than the proposed rent.

---

2. Ministry of Housing, Communities and Local Government, *Civil Penalties Statutory Guidance* (2025).

- Telling someone you have received other bids to encourage them to bid more than the proposed rent.
- Acting in a way that leads a person to believe they need to offer more than the proposed rent.
- Accepting an offer to pay more than the proposed rent, even if the landlord or agent didn't ask for it.

If a landlord or agent receives an offer from an applicant to pay more, they should say that they are unable to accept more than the proposed rent.

As with the obligation to specify the proposed rent, local councils have a duty to enforce the ban on rental bidding. They also have the same powers to investigate suspected breaches and impose civil penalties as with the proposed rent. However, the starting point in the statutory guidance is £4,000, which is £1,000 more than for failing to state the proposed rent.

5. Tenants' right to challenge initial rent

When setting the rent, landlords should bear in mind that tenants have the right under section 14 HA88 to challenge the rent in the first six months of a tenancy at the First-tier Tribunal (FTT). The FTT has the power to reduce the rent if they consider it to be above the "open-market rent" for a similar property in that area.

The open-market rent is the amount of rent a property could reasonably achieve if it were let today on the open market by a willing landlord to a willing tenant.

Keep evidence of how you decided on the proposed rent, together with examples of offers you received from other applicants that would support your decision to let the property for this rent. This may be useful evidence in the event the tenant does challenge the rent.

6. Prohibited pre-tenancy rent payments

The Renters' Rights Act introduced complex rules which ban rent payments before the tenancy agreement is entered into.

It is now a prohibited payment under the Tenant Fees Act 2019 for a "relevant person" to make a rent payment before the tenancy is entered into by both parties. It's also a breach of the TFA for a landlord or letting agent to ask, encourage or even accept an unsolicited payment of rent from a relevant person before the agreement is entered into.

What is a "relevant person"?

Section 1(9) TFA defines relevant person as "a tenant, or [...] a person acting on behalf of, or who has guaranteed the payment of rent by, a tenant". In other words, a relevant person is a tenant or a guarantor.

However, section 1(10) TFA excludes the local authorities and someone acting on their behalf from the definition of "relevant persons".

What this means is that a local authority is permitted to pay a landlord rent in advance to "facilitate a let" where the tenancy is agreed to meet the local authority's homelessness duty. The tenancy agreement can therefore legally include a clause requiring, for instance, the local authority to pay the landlord six months' rent in advance before the applicant signs and pay an additional lump sum of rent every six months.[3]

What does "entered into" mean?

The RRA doesn't explain what "entered into" means, so we need to look at English contract law, which says this is the point when the parties have reached a legally binding agreement, and acceptance of the terms has been communicated to the other parties.

From a practical point of view, this is when the parties have executed the agreement, and it is not "subject to contract" or the performance of any conditions.

This means that a landlord or letting agent must not ask for the tenant or their guarantor to make the first or any other rent payment until after the agreement is signed by all.

What if the tenant sends the rent before signing?

If the tenant pays the first rent payment along with their tenancy deposit, the landlord must return the rent payment.

This is because it is a breach of the TFA for a landlord or a letting agent to accept an unsolicited payment of rent for an assured periodic tenancy before the agreement is entered into.

7. Payment of the initial rent

Once the tenancy agreement has been entered into, the rules about rent in advance change.

---

3. See Ministry of Housing, Communities and Local Government, *Tenant Fees Act Statutory Guidance* (2025).

Permitted pre-tenancy period

The tenant may pay the rent for the first rent period (called the "initial rent") in the "permitted pre-tenancy period".

This is the time between all parties entering into the tenancy, and the start of the tenancy. This is the only time when a landlord can require a tenant to pay rent *before* the rent period to which it relates.

The amount payable for a rent period cannot be more than for any later rent periods, as the additional amount in the first payment would be a prohibited payment under the TFA.

It's possible for this initial rent to be for a rent period that is shorter than the rent periods during the tenancy; for instance, if the landlord prefers for the rent to be paid on a particular day of the month.

How much can the initial rent be?

Under the RRA, the initial rent payment cannot be more than the rent for one calendar month.

Consequently, since 1 May 2026, it has not been possible for the rent for the first rent period to be more than the usual monthly rent to dovetail with a standard rent payment date (e.g. the first of the month) or be payable after the tenant received their salary.

WORKED EXAMPLE

The tenancy starts on the 20th of the month, but the tenant wants to pay the rent on the 25th of the month as they get paid on the 24th of the month. The landlord is happy to agree to this, as it reduces the risk of rent arrears.

The initial rent cannot be one calendar month plus 5 days. Instead, the initial payment would need to be for the 5 days from the 20th to the 25th, with the second and subsequent rent periods to be from the 25th of each month.

Alternatively, the tenancy agreement could state that the rent payment date is the 25th of the month, which means it is paid five days into the rent period.

Now that we have gone through the rules about rent setting and collection before the tenancy starts, we will now look at how to find tenants without using a high street letting agent in Chapter 7.

CHAPTER 7

FINDING TENANTS USING ONLINE AGENTS

The overwhelming majority of renters find properties by searching the online portals such as Rightmove and Zoopla, and not by registering with individual letting agents.

As online agents such as OpenRent and Hello Neighbour make it simple for landlords to advertise their properties on the portals, it's never been easier for landlords to use these online agents to find tenants, bypassing traditional letting agents. I've not used traditional letting agents since I discovered online agents in 2022.

Here are the steps to follow to find tenants yourself, without using high street letting agents, saving yourself a considerable amount of money in the process.

1. Choose an online agent

Landlords cannot advertise directly on the property portals, such as Rightmove, Zoopla and On the Market, and need to use an online agent to do so.

Online agents provide many of the same services as traditional high street agents, but without local offices staffed with agents who do viewings. (That said, some online agents such as Hello Neighbour provide a viewings service as an optional extra.)

At their most basic, online agents allow landlords to list their rental properties on the property portals and provide a platform which enables landlords to communicate with applicants. When an applicant clicks through on an advertisement, they can contact the landlord through the online agent's platform and arrange a viewing.

The agents also offer other services such as the inventory, floor plans, professional photography, EPCs, referencing, the handling of the tenancy deposit, the creation of the tenancy and the service of safety certificates.

The market leader is OpenRent, and they offer a "no frills" listing service and a slightly more expensive tenant creation and advertising service called "Rent Now". Another option is Hello Neighbour, which offers similar services.

2. Decide on the proposed rent

The next step is to decide how much rent you would like to advertise the property for, following the principles set out in Chapter 6.

As explained, for APTs, you must state the proposed rent in your advertising and listings and won't be able to ask an applicant to pay more than the proposed rent or to accept an unsolicited higher rent.

3. How to market your property

Advertising on the property portals helps you attract as many high-quality applicants as possible. However, many rental listings are poor, without decent photos, a floor plan or a video, which give a negative impression.

It is worth putting time and effort into how you present your properties on the portals, as this will increase the odds of a great applicant clicking on "arrange a viewing" and give you a better selection of suitable applicants to choose from.

Let potential renters see how your property flows. Will it work for them? Giving them the information they need will help weed out time-wasters. It will also encourage out-of-towners to make the journey to view the property.

Here are some tips on how to make your property stand out on the portals and attract great renters:

Create a compelling property description

The online agent's platform will guide you through creating the property description and the terms of the tenancy on offer; for instance, the pet policy, number of tenants, deposit amount, etc.

If you don't feel comfortable with writing your own property description, the platforms can generate one for you using AI, but I would edit it carefully to make sure it doesn't sound like AI, with overstatements such as "critical" and "exceptional".

Ensure the property description includes the material information

The Digital Markets, Competition and Consumers Act 2024 (DMCCA) requires landlords to ensure that the listing contains sufficient "material information" so that a prospective tenant can make an informed decision about whether or not to arrange a viewing, put in an offer to rent or go ahead with renting the property.

At the date of publication, there is no official guidance as to exactly what information needs to be included in listings to let a property.

This is because the DMCCA superseded and replaced the Consumer Protection from Unfair Trading Regulations 2008 (CPRs) with effect from 6 April 2025. The previous guidance for letting agents on what material information should be included in listings, which was based on the CPRs, was withdrawn shortly afterwards.[1]

Since then, nothing has been forthcoming about what constitutes material information for lettings, although an MHCLG consultation on developing guidance for the selling process said they would "return to the possibility of similar guidance for residential letting agents at a later stage".[2]

Checklist for property descriptions

In the absence of official guidance, and taking a common-sense approach, here is a list of information to include in the property description that would help a potential tenant decide whether to view a rental property, put in an offer or actually rent the property.

---

1. The previous guidance was National Trading Standards, *Material Information in Property Listings (Lettings): Guidance for Letting Agents*, November 2023, and it was withdrawn in May 2025. The latest information is available at: https://www.nationaltradingstandards.uk/work-areas/estate-agency-team/material-information.
2. Ministry of Housing, Communities and Local Government, *Consultation Material Information in Property Listings* (2025), https://www.gov.uk/government/consultations/material-information-in-property-listings.

- The proposed rent and the applicable rent period (e.g. weekly or per calendar month).
- If bills are included, the listing should specify which bills these are.
- Council tax band.
- EPC rating number and graphic.
- Details of the deposit and any holding deposit that the landlord requires.
- Property type (flat, terraced house, semi-detached house, detached house, etc).
- For flats in a larger building, the floor of the flat, e.g. ground floor.
- The number of bedrooms.
- The broadband speed.[3] (The platform may include this automatically).
- Any known problems with mobile phone signal.
- Details of any parking available, e.g. residents' parking, off-street parking, on-street parking.
- Building safety risks (unsafe cladding, presence of asbestos, unsafe flooring, etc).
- Flood and coastal erosion risks.

Take lovely photos

In order to attract the best tenants, it is worth investing in quality photography. A minimum of ten photos is a good rule of thumb for a three-bedroom house.

While the online platforms offer an option for professional photography, it is possible to take photos yourself (I share some tips in the box below). Be sure to move the bins and

3. See Ofcom, *Broadband Checker*, https://checker.ofcom.org.uk/en-gb/broadband-coverage.

general clutter out of the way for the exterior shots and make sure it's tidy and uncluttered inside.

PHOTOGRAPHY TIPS

For the best results, use a camera and a tripod so that the photos are from the same height. It is possible to take photos on a mobile phone, but I would recommend investing in an inexpensive tripod for the phone.

A tripod height at 4.5 ft (chest/midriff level) means the camera will capture equal amounts of floor and ceiling. If it's at eye level, there's too much ceiling. The tripod can be a little higher in the kitchen, so the photos show the surface of the counter tops.

Shoot the photos in landscape mode. There is no need to have a wide-angle lens.

Use the timer on the camera so you can put the camera in the far corner and leave the room to avoid being in shot to achieve the widest possible shot with a standard lens.

If you don't have special lighting equipment, take the interior photos around midday, when the light is best.

You can edit the photos in Lightroom to even out the lighting. You can also do this in Canva if you don't have an Adobe subscription.

Prepare a floor plan

I highly recommend preparing a floor plan, as prospective tenants like to understand how the property flows. Even a standard Victorian house has so many variations, and it's useful for potential renters to see how it is laid out.

The online portals offer a floor plan service, but it is possible to do it yourself online.[4] You can use a laser measure for ease and speed.

Film a simple video

Relatively few letting agents do video tours for rental properties, even at the top end of the market in London.

You can easily make your property stand out on the portals and help potential tenants decide whether to view the property, by making a simple video on your phone.

For Rightmove, you need to upload a horizontal video with a 16:9 ratio onto YouTube and then embed a link into the listing.

A short 60-second video works well, speeding up the tour and editing it so it lingers in the main rooms and not, say, the stairs. Show the view outside if it's nice! The video doesn't need to be too fancy. Applicants appreciate it as they get a better feel for the property before attending the viewing.

4. Handling enquiries from applicants

The viewing and enquiry organiser on most online platforms makes it easy to communicate with potential applicants, without giving them a mobile phone number or email address. You can message the applicants via the platform to ask further questions, organise viewings on the platform, and send invitations to view the property.

4. For instance, Metropix, https://www.landmark.co.uk/products/metropix.

In order to remove unsuitable applicants from the process, I recommend setting up automatic screening, which requires applicants to say whether they meet each of the criteria when they request a viewing. It saves a lot of time to have all viewing requests come through with the proposed move-in date, combined monthly income, whether they have a pet, etc. For another layer of screening, you can create your own Tenant Auto-Reply email to be sent at the same time.

See below for examples of screening questions for the Auto-Reply email to help you find long-term tenants and eliminate intermediaries such as rent-to-renters:

SCREENING QUESTIONS FOR AUTO-REPLY

Please state the occupation of any adults who would live there.

Please confirm the income of each adult.

How many adults and how many children would live in the property? What are the ages of the children?

What are the breeds and age of any pets (if applicable)?

Where do you live now and why are you looking to move?

What is your connection to [town]?

How long are you planning to live in this property?

Have you or any of the other adults ever had any CCJs? If so, please provide details.

Is the property for yourself? If not, explain why you are asking to view for someone else. Please do not apply if you are a rent-to-renter or another intermediary.

If you're happy with the answers, contact the applicant through the platform to arrange a viewing. The platform should send them a message with the details of the address.

It's usually possible to use the platform to ask more questions, reject an application or arrange a call to clarify some answers.

Keep all communications on the platform to protect your privacy, and to ensure that there is an independent, permanent record, as WhatsApp messages can be deleted.

Remember that you cannot refuse to allow applicants who receive benefits or have a family to view the property, unless you have a legitimate reason to refuse, as this will be rental discrimination, which I explain in Chapter 2.

5. How to carry out viewings

Viewings when the property is empty

As I have long-term tenants, I prefer to do viewings after the previous tenants have left, so I can carry out repairs or maintenance and ensure the property is thoroughly clean before I start the viewings. It's surprising how much grubbier things look without furniture.

Although this approach means I may have a void for an additional few weeks, I believe the advantages outweigh the slight loss of rental income.

Another advantage of arranging viewings when a property is empty is that it's easy to do them when it's convenient for you.

In order to avoid multiple visits to the property, you can group viewings together for an evening or at the weekend and offer 15-minute slots to applicants. T his approach is a good use of your time, and it helps applicants see there is competition for the property. A good rule of thumb is to book viewings at 15-minute intervals.

Viewings when a tenant is still living there

If you wish to minimise the time when the property or room is empty, you may decide to conduct viewings while your tenant is still living there. This can be tricky, and you'll need to agree viewing times with them before you can confirm viewings.

They can refuse to allow viewings, but they're less likely to do so if you've been reasonable with them. For instance, agreeing blocks of time for viewings with them before you advertise will reduce the disruption for them.

Preparing for the viewings

Safety first

As the sad case of the disappearance of estate agent Suzy Lamplugh in 1986 showed us, conducting viewings can be dangerous.

Safety is paramount. While incidents are rare, it is sensible to take precautions. It's best not to do viewings by yourself, but sometimes that cannot be avoided. I have set out a few tips in the box below to help you keep safe should you need to show tenants around your property yourself:

TIPS TO KEEP SAFE DURING VIEWINGS

Don't let applicants know in advance that you'll be by

yourself. For instance, you can say "we look forward to meeting you".

Take a charged phone with Find My Friends (or similar) enabled. Keep it in your pocket as you go round the property.

Arrange the viewings on the platform, so that there's an independent record of the meeting. Let someone know who you will be meeting and when you expect to finish.

Try to arrange viewings in daytime hours if possible.

Arranging multiple viewings 15 minutes apart can also help personal safety, as it means you won't be alone for long before the next applicant arrives.

Don't leave the keys to the property or your car on display. Keep them with you.

Let the applicant go up the stairs first, but come down the stairs yourself first, so you are always closest to the entrance.

Send reminders

The platform is likely to send reminders automatically, but if you're arranging viewings yourself, do send reminders and ask them to confirm they're coming. You might have someone on the waiting list for a slot who can come instead.

Get there early to prepare the property

Whether or not the property is empty, do get there early to turn on the heating or open windows to air the rooms, depending on the weather. You can clear away accumulated post, and have a little tidy up, if need be. If work is being done to the property, make sure it's safe to walk around.

I always pick up rubbish in the street and in the front garden, to improve the kerb appeal. Check the back garden to see if anything needs a hasty tidy up.

If there's no off-street parking, it's a good idea to park a short walk away to free up a parking space near the property.

Carrying out viewings

How to conduct the viewing

It can be a bit intimidating carrying out viewings, as it's a two-way interview process. You're sizing up the applicants, and they're trying to decide whether the property is right for them, as well as whether you're a good landlord.

There's no magic order to show the rooms and it depends on the layout of your property and your preferences. Give them lots of opportunity to ask questions and offer to let them go around the property again by themselves.

What to talk about during viewings?

Viewings provide an excellent opportunity to try to get the measure of those who you may be entering into a long-term business relationship with. Following the abolition of section 21 no fault evictions, landlords need to be even more careful over tenant selection, as it's now more difficult to evict unsuitable tenants.

I chat with each of them as they go round, asking open questions, to get a sense of what they're looking for. I ask myself if they will be good tenants who'll be happy in the house and stay a long time. Or does it feel like a stopgap?

Questions to ask during viewings

Here are some of the questions I ask to try to understand their motivations, before I follow up with references. I do this informally as I do the viewing. These questions build on the screening questions.

- Where are you living currently and why are you looking to move?
- How long have you lived there? And the place before?
- Where do you work? How will you get there from here? What's the journey like? How often do you work from home?
- How long have you worked for your company?
- What do you like about this property?
- What attracts you to this area? Do you have any family or friends nearby?
- How long are you looking to rent the property?
- Tell me about your pet(s). (A very leading question). How often do you leave the pet alone at home?
- Do you have a good credit record? Any CCJs?
- Have you ever paid rent late? If so, why, and when did you make up the arrears? What would their current landlord or letting agent say about them?
- Would anyone else be staying at the property regularly? (Remember you can't discriminate against applicants who regularly have children to stay, unless the property is unsuitable for children).

What to say at the end of the viewing

At the end of the viewing, explain what the process is if they're interested in proceeding, assuming you're happy for them to proceed. Although you are likely to have pre-screened the applicants before the viewings, some may not have been telling the full truth.

Ask them to contact you via the platform to say whether they wish to proceed, and when they would like to move in.

In order to manage expectations, explain that you'll be creating a shortlist of those applicants who wish to proceed, and will be in touch to let them know if they're on the shortlist. Let them know that once you have made a decision, you will take a holding deposit from one set of applicants and take them through full referencing and credit checks. If the first on the list aren't successful, you'll go to the next set of applicants.

Finally, remind them they'd need to pass the affordability criteria of a household income including benefits of at least 2.5 x the rent, and that you'll carry out full referencing and credit checks before entering into a tenancy agreement.

For landlords who accept applicants who don't meet the affordability criteria, they should mention the requirements for guarantors (good credit history and a salary that is at least 4 x the rent). Landlords can no longer require tenants to pay rent in advance, e.g. 6 or 12 months' rent.

Now that we have a shortlist of pre-screened prospective tenants, we turn to the vetting and final selection of the tenants in Chapter 8.

CHAPTER 8

TENANT SELECTION AND VETTING

Choosing good tenants is probably the single most important thing for landlords.

Good tenants make being a landlord relatively straightforward. Problematic tenants, on the other hand, can make the lives of their landlords, letting agents and neighbours a misery. Also, because of delays in the court system, it is usually time-consuming both to evict bad tenants (especially now section 21 has been abolished) and to recover rent arrears. Prevention is better than cure.

In this chapter, I give lots of practical tips on what to look for when you're selecting and vetting tenants, whether you do this directly yourselves or use a letting agent to help you.

1. What is a good tenant?

These are the three questions I ask myself about the applicants when I'm making my selection:

Will they pay the rent on time and in full?

This is of fundamental importance. Good tenants honour their side of the tenancy agreement, which includes paying the rent in full and on time. In return, good landlords hold up their end of the bargain by providing well-maintained properties for them to live in.

Affordability is very important. I look for tenants whose joint income including benefits is at least 2.5 times the rent, and I include the figure in my advertisements.

Although I'm a responsible landlord and care about the wellbeing of those who live in my buy-to-lets, being a landlord is ultimately a business. I don't want to have to chase rent payments or take tenants to court for rent arrears. Also, I don't want to have to evict tenants because of rent arrears.

One way of reducing the risk is by avoiding renters with a history of rent arrears. If a prospective tenant had rent arrears during the pandemic, I'd expect them to be upfront about it. I would be reasonable about genuine cases. However, if they don't disclose arrears which later show up in the reference, I'll turn them down.

If there's any doubt about affordability, it's a good idea to ask for someone to guarantee their rent or for them to arrange a professional guarantor.

Will they look after the property properly?

It's important for tenants to look after the property properly. This means that they should keep the inside and outside of the property clean, maintain the garden and dispose of rubbish properly. They also need to do basic maintenance tasks like clearing out hair from shower traps.

Part of looking after the property properly is letting the landlord or agent know when something needs repairing. This includes repairs such as a slow leak or a hazardous situation.

It's also important that tenants give access to the landlord and their contractors to carry out maintenance and repairs.

Will they be a good neighbour?

I wouldn't let to anyone if I had good grounds to believe they wouldn't be a good neighbour, as being a good neighbour is part of being a good tenant. Being a good neighbour also includes being a good person to live with in an HMO.

What do I mean by a good neighbour? It's someone who treats their neighbours with respect and doesn't engage in anti-social behaviour such as making excessive noise, being abusive, fighting or vandalism.

Taking care to choose tenants that are likely to be good neighbours is also part of being a good landlord. Neighbours are important. I always give my card to the neighbours either side of my buy-to-lets. They can be an early warning system of problems with tenants.

2. How to choose between applicants

Regardless of whether you use letting agents to compile a shortlist of applicants or do it yourself, you're likely to need to make a choice between different applicants. You should also vet them thoroughly before coming to a final decision.

In this section, I share what to look out for, and what to disregard when choosing between applicants.

What should landlords look for in tenants?

As well as the basics discussed above, any additional selection criteria will depend on what type of tenant you're looking for.

Single lets

For single let houses which are suitable for families, look for long-term tenants who will put down roots and stay, so you have minimal voids. This also makes it easier for landlords to manage their portfolios themselves.

As I look for long-term renters, I prefer locals or people with good reasons for wanting to live in the area, as they're more likely to be happy and stay. I'm not interested in people passing through.

HMOs

A landlord of an HMO, on the other hand, will have additional or different priorities, as they're choosing people from different households to live with each other.

The group dynamics of the house or flat need to be right. The last thing an HMO landlord wants is to introduce a new person into the house who doesn't get on with the others and causes the others to leave. They may give priority to those of similar age or the same sex as the current tenants, or those who work similar hours.

Some HMO landlords will even give a shortlist to the other tenants to interview and choose from, once they meet the affordability criteria.

What can't landlords take into account when selecting tenants?

Landlords do not have complete freedom to choose or reject whoever they like.

The Equality Act 2010 makes it illegal for landlords to discriminate against applicants because of their nationality, race, religion or disability. It also prohibits landlords from rejecting applicants based on their sex, sexual orientation or gender reassignment.

Additionally, as explained in Chapter 2, the RRA makes it specifically illegal to discriminate against applicants who have children or who are benefit claimants. This is called "rental discrimination". The local housing authority can also impose a penalty of up to £7,000 if they are satisfied "on a balance of probabilities" that the landlord or agent discriminated against applicants because of their benefit status or because they have children.

Also, it is possible to get rent guarantee insurance with applicants who receive benefits. What matters is whether they can afford the rent and are likely to pay the rent in full and on time. Their credit history is a good way of predicting whether they'll manage their money sufficiently well to keep up to date with the rent.

Don't base your selection on discriminatory criteria. Not only will they have no bearing over whether the person will be a good tenant, but it's illegal.

Why your gut feel is important

Gut feel is an under-rated way to choose between applicants There may well be a good reason for feeling uneasy about applicants.

Here are a few questions to ask yourself:

- Do they seem decent and reasonable?
- Do you trust them to look after your property, pay the rent on time and be good neighbours?
- Does anything they say not quite add up?
- Are they pushy?
- Are they polite?
- If they were late, did they message you to tell you and have a plausible reason?
- Would you be happy to live next door to them?
- How do they speak to their partner and/or any children?

3. Tenant application form

Applicants should fill in a formal application before you or your agent carry out full referencing checks. When I say "applicants", this means every adult who would be living at the property, even if they're not contributing to the rent. For instance, an adult child in full-time education.

Some self-letting landlords ask all applicants to fill in the form before they view a property. I think this is overkill, and means the landlord ends up with personal data they don't strictly need.

I therefore only ask applicants to fill in the application form once I have made a preliminary decision to go forward with an application. I don't want all of that personal information about applicants who, for whatever reason, don't proceed to the next stage.

Once you receive the completed application form, go through it closely to see if there is anything that makes you conclude you don't want to rent to them after all. Doing it at this stage means you can reject the applicant before you ask for a holding deposit or spend money on referencing. It also means you can go to the next applicant on the list.

4. How to reference tenants

Thorough referencing is one of the most important steps in the letting process.

Applicants sometimes don't tell the truth and hope the landlord or agent won't ask for references, so don't be tempted to skip or shortcut the referencing process, even if someone is desperate to move in straight away.

I've had several applicants give me blatantly false information, and I was able to reject them when I got the referencing reports. It was money well spent.

Here are a few tips to carry out thorough referencing:

Professional referencing and credit checks

Professional referencing is key to making sure someone is who they say they are, can afford the rent and have a track record of showing they will pay the rent in full and on time. You will also need this to qualify for rent guarantee insurance for new tenants.

The report can be up to 10–15 pages, depending on the provider. It includes a previous landlord reference, verified sources of income and an employment check, and will give an affordability rating.

The report will also have a credit check, CCJ check, linked addresses and fraud information. They typically include the contact details of the previous landlord/letting agent and employer, which make it easy to follow up if there are any issues (for instance, rent arrears). The level of detail in the report makes it simple to cross-reference with the tenant application form.

If you use a letting agent, make sure they obtain full professional references so that you will qualify for rent guarantee insurance.

There are many companies that provide formal referencing checks for self-letting landlords. It's not expensive, and it's a false economy not to do it. You'll also need to have carried out professional referencing to claim on rent guarantee insurance for new tenants.

Referencing will be listed as an optional extra on the online platforms such as OpenRent and Hello Neighbour, or you can go direct to The Lettings Hub as they offer a "direct to landlord" service. At the date of publication, the NRLA offers referencing direct to landlords in collaboration with Goodlord.[1]

---

1. NRLA, *Tenant Referencing,* https://www.nrla.org.uk/services/tenant-checks/your-references.

Landlord references

The standard referencing service will provide a reference from the most recent landlord, but that landlord might not tell the whole truth if they want the tenant to move out. It's therefore wise to ask to speak to the previous landlord or agent, as they might be more forthcoming. I say "speak" deliberately.

People tend to give away more information on the phone, even if it's what they don't say. A pause or a sigh can reveal a lot! Have a chat with them, if they're willing, and probe a little. You can ask to speak to the previous landlord, even if you use letting agents.

Do watch out for fake landlords and agents, as applicants do sometimes provide contact details of fake landlords and agents. It's easier to do this on the phone, to get a feel for whether the person you're speaking to is really a landlord or an agent.

You can use the information on the tenant application form and the results of the credit check (which list previous addresses), to check what the landlord or agent says. Ask for the dates of the tenancy, details of rent increases and why they moved out.

Your own checks

Don't rely solely on the professional referencing and credit checks, but do your own checks as well, even if you use letting agents. Social media and Google can be great ways to find out information on your applicants. You can check whether their social media profiles tally with what your applicants tell you about themselves.

LinkedIn is valuable for showing if they change jobs regularly, or if there are unexplained gaps in employment. On the plus side, it can reveal steady promotions within the same company. Any posts can give an insight into them as a person. Facebook and Instagram can reveal their priorities and life choices – it's surprising just how much information some people reveal about themselves on social media.

Google can be a treasure trove, revealing failed businesses, complaints and even newspaper reports.

Some landlords arrange to do the Right to Rent checks at the tenants' current property as a final check to see how they look after their current home. This is particularly useful if they have pets.

5. Right to rent checks

Right to rent refers to the obligation on landlords to check that all tenants, permitted occupiers and lodgers aged 18 or over who will live in the property are not disqualified from renting a property because of their immigration status.

The checks need to be carried out even if the person is not listed as a tenant on the tenancy agreement. (References to tenants for the purposes of the Right to Rent include permitted occupiers and lodgers.)

If a prospective or current tenant cannot prove their right to rent, they cannot move into the rental property.

Landlords can delegate the Right to Rent checks to a letting agent or to a certified Identity Service Provider (IDSP). IDSPs are authorised to validate the identity and right to rent of

British and Irish nationals on behalf of a landlord. However, it's also possible for landlords to do it themselves.

Be aware that the rules change regularly, so you should always check the latest rules on GOV.UK before carrying out the Right to Rent checks.[2]

Whose Right to Rent must be checked?

Landlords must check all adults, even if they "seem" British. It's against the law to only check people you think are not British citizens. You must not discriminate against anyone because of where they were born or make assumptions about their nationality based on their accent or appearance.

Not everyone with a British accent is British, and many British nationals have other accents. The only way not to discriminate is to treat all applicants the same, regardless of whether you believe them to be British.

How to carry out the Right to Rent checks

Checking the Right to Rent of British and Irish citizens

If the applicant is a British or Irish citizen, they can provide one of the following Group 1 documents to prove their right to rent:

- a British passport (current or expired)
- an Irish passport or passport card (current or expired)

2. See GOV.UK, *Checking your Tenant's Right to Rent*, https://www.gov.uk/check-tenant-right-to-rent-documents and this useful online form, *Check if Someone Can Rent Your Residential Property*, https://www.gov.uk/landlord-immigration-check.

- a certificate of registration or naturalisation as a British citizen

If they don't have any of the above documents, they can prove their right to rent by providing two of the following documents from Group 2:

- a current UK driving licence (full or provisional).
- a full birth or adoption certificate from the UK, Guernsey, Jersey, the Isle of Man or Ireland.
- a letter from their employer within the last three months.
- a letter from a British passport holder in an "accepted profession".
- a letter from a UK Government department or local council.
- proof they currently get benefits.
- a letter from a British school, college, or university that they currently go to.
- a Disclosure and Barring Service (DBS) certificate.
- proof that they have served in the UK Armed Forces.
- a letter within the last three months from a private rented sector access scheme or a voluntary organisation that's helping them with housing.
- a letter confirming they have been released from prison within the past six months.
- a letter confirming their probation from their offender manager from within the last three months.
- a letter within the last three months from the UK police about the theft of their passport.

Checking the Right to Rent of other nationalities

Ask to see their passport so you can check their likeness, and take a copy of their passport data page. Then you will need to see they have the right to rent in the UK by checking their share code or their original immigration documents:

Share code

A share code is a 9-character code that allows a landlord to look up someone's right to rent when they're not a British or Irish citizen. It's an easy way to check the right to rent of other nationalities.

You will need the share code and date of birth to be able to look it up on GOV.UK.[3] The prospective tenant needs to apply online for the code and provide it with their date of birth to their landlord. The code is valid for 90 days.

Immigration documents

If the person doesn't have a share code, the landlord can check their immigration documents to see if they have the right to rent.

As the rules are very complex, it's best to use the process on the GOV.UK webpage (see above) to find out which documents give someone the right to rent and how to check them.

Landlords can also call the Home Office helpline: 0300 790 6268.

---

3. See *Check a Tenant's Right to Rent in England: Use Their Share Code*, https://www.gov.uk/view-right-to-rent.

How long should Right to Rent records be kept?

Landlords (or agents) should keep copies of the documents checked for the duration of the tenancy agreement or lodger's agreement, and for at least one year afterwards.

How often should the Right to Rent be checked?

Tenants with a permanent right to rent

If tenants have a permanent right to rent, including British and Irish citizens, landlords only need to check the documents once, before the original tenancy starts.

There's no need to check the right to rent again if the tenancy is renewed and the tenant has a permanent right to rent.

Tenants with a time-limited right to rent

Tenants who are not British or Irish may have valid immigration permission for a limited period. This includes pre-settled status via the EU Settlement Scheme, or time-limited permission under the points-based immigration system.

Landlords should do a follow-up check of a time-limited right to rent before 12 months have passed or, if the time-limited right to rent expires after a 12-month period, then before the right to rent expires.

They must make a report to the Home Office if they become aware that a renter has lost or is about to lose their right to rent. The form will generate a unique reference number which you should keep. Landlords must make the report as soon as reasonably possible and before the existing time-limited statutory excuse expires.

A correct Right to Rent check will protect the landlord from prosecution for at least 12 months. Landlords only need to perform a follow-up check 10 or 11 months after their previous Right to Rent check.

If the landlord doesn't do a follow-up check, they could receive a civil penalty (see below). If the tenant fails a follow-up check, and the landlord doesn't report it to the Home Office, the landlord could be sent to prison for up to five years.

Minors turning 18

There is no requirement to check the right to rent of a minor. If a minor turns 18 years of age during a tenancy, they are permitted to continue living there, and the landlord isn't required to carry out a Right to Rent check when the child turns 18 years of age.

However, where follow-up checks are required for the other existing tenants, the now adult should be included in those checks when they are due.

Civil penalties for breaching the Right to Rent rules

Landlords can receive tough civil penalties if they rent their property to someone who is not allowed to stay in the UK and they cannot show they checked their right to rent. This is why it's so important to keep full records.

The penalty is £10,000 per tenant for a first offence. For a repeat offence, it is £20,000 per person.

Landlords can object to a penalty within 28 days of the "given" date on the civil penalty notice, for instance where a tenant no longer has a right to rent but the landlord either made a correct check on the tenant or reported it to the Home Office after a repeat check. There is a further right of appeal.

6. Checklist for vetting tenants

In summary, here are the key green and red flags to have in mind when you are vetting applicants with a view to selecting good tenants. It's beyond simply looking at a credit history but is about looking at the wider picture to decide whether this is someone who will make a good tenant.

Green flags

These are things that reassure me that the applicants might make good tenants:

- Good steady jobs, with the household income at least 2.5 x the rent.
- Presentable, turn up on time, polite and not overly familiar.
- Ask good questions about the house, maintenance and area.
- Good reason for leaving current home.
- Good reason for wanting to live in this area.
- Their household isn't too big for the property.
- Good references from employers and previous landlords/letting agents.
- No CCJs and a good credit record; open and honest about any previous issues.

Red flags

Here are the things that would concern me about applicants and make me think they might not make good tenants. I might overlook one or two red flags if the applicants have a good explanation, but I would reject them if they lied or were aggressive or rude.

- Previous history of rent arrears without a good explanation.
- Poor credit history without a good reason.
- Frequent job changes without a good explanation.
- Lying or misrepresenting something to you, e.g. saying they have no previous rent arrears or CCJs, when they do.
- Asking to sub-let. I want all adults to be joint tenants on the tenancy agreement, and don't allow sub-letting.
- Wanting to cut corners or break the law, e.g. offering above the advertised rent or trying to pay advance rent before you both sign, both of which would be a breach of the Tenant Fees Act.
- Saying they need to move in urgently.
- Being generally pushy.
- Wanting two households in a single let in an area with additional licensing, making it a licensable HMO.
- Being cagey about giving landlord or employer references.
- Having unexplained gaps in rental history that appear in the credit report which they never mentioned.
- Being overly and unreasonably demanding during the viewing or after.

- Reacting badly when told about six-monthly maintenance checks.
- Reacting badly when asked questions.
- Shouting and swearing at their partner or children.
- Being evasive about their pets. (Most pet owners are only too happy to show off photos on their phone of their adored pets!)
- Making racist, sexist or other inappropriate comments.
- Being rude about the neighbours or the area generally.
- You feel uncomfortable with them.

Once you are ready to proceed with your chosen tenants, you will need to set up the new tenancy, which is the subject of Chapter 9.

CHAPTER 9

SETTING UP A NEW TENANCY

In this chapter, I go through what you need to know about setting up the tenancy, from explaining what fees landlords and letting agents can charge tenants, to the handling of the holding deposit, the tenancy agreement, whether you may need a guarantor, and your obligations regarding tenancy deposits.

1. Tenant fees

The Tenant Fees Act 2019 (TFA) strictly regulates what landlords and agents can charge tenants both when setting up the tenancy and throughout the tenancy for assured periodic tenancies and licences to occupy. Schedule 1 and associated guidance set out the payments that are permitted.[1] If a payment or a fee is not on the list, it is "prohibited".

Note that the TFA does not apply to high rent tenancies (where the rent is more than £100,000 a year), as they are not within the definition of "tenancy" in section 28 TFA.

1. Ministry of Housing, Communities and Local Government, *Tenant Fees Act 2019: Guidance* (2020), https://www.gov.uk/government/publications/tenant-fees-act-2019-guidance and Ministry of Housing, Communities and Local Government, *Tenant Fees Act amended by the Renters' Rights Act 2025*. Statutory Guidance (2025), https://www.gov.uk/government/publications/tenant-fees-act-amended-by-the-renters-rights-act-2025.

First, I go through those payments that are permitted, before listing the payments that are prohibited under the TFA.

Permitted payments

Schedule 1 of the TFA sets out "permitted payments" which landlords and agents are permitted to charge tenants.

Here is an overview of the permitted payments:

Rent

Rent is generally a permitted payment under the TFA, in that once the landlord (or the agent on their behalf) and the tenant have signed the tenancy agreement, the landlord may ask for and receive payments of rent from the tenant.

This includes payment for the first rent period, of up to one calendar month's rent, which section 4B HA88 specifically states may be payable in the "permitted pre-tenancy period" between signing and the start of the tenancy.

It is, however, a breach of the TFA for landlords and agents to ask for rent to be paid before the tenancy agreement is signed. It is also a breach to accept rent before all parties have signed the tenancy agreement.

Rent should be payable at regular intervals and equally split across the tenancy, and landlords and agents must not charge tenants rent that is higher in earlier months than in later months. For instance, it is a prohibited payment to charge £800 per calendar month for months 1 to 10, and then £500 for months 11 and 12.

Refundable holding deposit

Landlords and agents may charge a refundable holding deposit to reserve a property, capped at one week's rent. I explain the rules about holding deposits in more detail below.

Refundable tenancy deposit

Landlords and agents may ask the tenant to pay a refundable tenancy deposit which is up to five weeks' rent for properties where the annual rent is below £50,000.

For tenancies with an annual rent of £50,000 or higher, a landlord or agent can ask for a tenancy deposit of up to six weeks' rent. Where the annual rent is over £100,000, the landlord or agent may ask for more, as high rent tenancies are not subject to the TFA, as mentioned above.

Default fee for late payment of rent

A landlord or agent may charge a tenant interest if rent has been outstanding for 14 days or more, provided the tenancy agreement states the landlord may do so.

The default fee must not be more than an annual percentage rate of 3% above the Bank of England's base rate, calculated on a daily basis.

Default payments for lost keys, security devices or fobs

If a tenant loses a key, security device or fob, a landlord or agent can charge a fee to replace it, provided this fee is set out in the tenancy agreement.

However, the charge must be reasonable, and the landlord or agent must provide evidence of the cost.

Changes to tenancy agreements

Landlords and agents can charge for certain changes to tenancy agreements; for instance, an assignment from one tenant to another (change of sharer), adding a tenant or providing consent to sub-let.

The charge should not ordinarily exceed £50, unless it is reasonable to charge more in the circumstances.

Council Tax

It is usual for tenants in a single let or joint tenancy to pay council tax directly to the relevant local authority if it is not included in the rent. For HMOs let by the room, the landlord is responsible for paying council tax.

The tenancy agreement or a written statement of terms must set it out clearly.

Payments for utilities

The tenancy agreement should clearly state which bills for electricity, gas or other fuel, water or sewerage are included in the rent.

With single lets, it is usual for tenants to be responsible for paying for utilities, landlines, broadband and water directly to the provider.

However, with HMOs or flats in a building owned by the landlord, the landlord may wish to pay these and either include it in the rent or set out details for a separate payment from the tenant to the landlord for these costs.

Landlords and agents not only cannot make a profit on utilities, but they also cannot charge more than their reasonable costs in providing a bill-paying service.

Again, details regarding bill payments must be spelt out in the tenancy agreement or in a standalone written statement of terms.

Television Licence

A landlord can include a payment for a TV Licence within the rent where this is agreed in the tenancy agreement.

However, if it's not included in the rent, landlords cannot charge tenants separately for this. If payments for a TV Licence are not included in the rent, a landlord can require the tenant to pay the TV Licence themselves.

Prohibited payments

Under the TFA, if a payment does not fall within the definition of "permitted payments" in Schedule 1, it will be a prohibited payment.

The *2025 Guidance*[2] confirms that it is prohibited for landlords and agents to do the following:

---

2. Ministry of Housing, Communities and Local Government, *Tenant Fees Act 2019: Statutory Guidance for Enforcement Authorities* (2025), https://www.gov.uk/government/publications/tenant-fees-act-amended-by-the-renters-rights-act-2025/tenant-fees-act-2019-statutory-guidance-for-enforcement-authorities.

- Ask for or encourage tenants to pay rent before the tenancy is entered into.
- Accept a rent payment before the tenancy is entered into.
- Charge tenants to view a property.
- Charge tenants to set up a tenancy; for instance, charging fees to set up a tenancy, referencing, arranging an inventory and administering the tenancy deposit.
- Require tenants to take out insurance.
- Require tenants to pay for chimney sweeping services.
- Charge separately for gardening services (although this can be included in the rent).
- Charge tenants for check-out fees, including a check-out inventory.
- Require tenants to use professional cleaners or professional carpet cleaning at the end of the tenancy. They can, however, require tenants to clean to a "professional standard" to return the property in the same state of cleanliness as they found it at the start of the tenancy.
- Charge tenants if the condition of the property changes as a result of fair wear and tear for the number of permitted occupants and authorised pets.

2. Handling the holding deposit

When the landlord or letting agent have chosen a preferred applicant they wish to proceed to referencing with, it's usual practice to ask for a holding deposit to reserve the property.

However, the handling of holding deposits is highly regulated, and a breach of the rules can lead to a steep penalty under the Tenant Fees Act 2019 (TFA).

As mentioned above, the rules in the TFA do not apply to high rent tenancies where the annual rent is over £100,000.

What is a holding deposit?

A holding deposit is a refundable payment which an applicant makes to show they are serious about wanting to rent a property. It "holds" the property for them while referencing takes place and the tenancy agreement is prepared.

The TFA prohibits holding deposits from being more than one week's rent. Round down to the nearest £1, so you don't inadvertently go over the one-week limit.

Under the TFA, landlords and letting agents can't take more than one holding deposit at a time and must not show any further applicants the property unless the application is unsuccessful.

Once an applicant pays a holding deposit, the landlord or agent have two weeks to enter a tenancy agreement with the applicant, unless they agree an extension period with the tenant in writing. If not, they must return the holding deposit.

The Government guidance states that landlords should provide the applicants with clear information about the tenancy itself, including a draft tenancy agreement and the circumstances which might cause them to lose the holding deposit, before the landlord or letting agent accepts the holding deposit.[3]

---

3. *Tenant Fees Act 2019: Guidance for Landlords and Agents* (2020), p.33.

This means that landlords and agents must clearly explain their suitability requirements to applicants before taking the holding deposit, such as the minimum income, a clean credit history with no CCJs and no false or misleading information.

When can a landlord or letting agent keep a holding deposit?

Here is a summary of circumstances when the landlord or agent can keep the holding deposit, as set out in Schedule 2 of the TFA:

- The applicant provides false or misleading information, and this materially affects their suitability as a tenant. A landlord or agent must be able to prove that they have actively lied; for instance, if they state on the tenant application form, they've never had CCJs, but a credit check shows they did. This is why it's so important to have a tenant application form, as it is written evidence that they provided false or misleading information if it differs from that received during referencing and credit checks.
- The applicant decides not to proceed with the tenancy.
- The applicant doesn't take "all reasonable steps" to proceed with the tenancy. For instance, they don't provide or are slow in providing contact details for a landlord or employer reference. However, this doesn't include a situation where the tenant provides the contact details of their current landlord, but that landlord is slow.
- The applicant fails the Right to Rent check.

Landlords and agents are not entitled to keep the holding deposit if the applicant "fails" referencing, only if the applicant provided materially false or misleading information.

Assuming the landlord or letting agent has grounds to keep a holding deposit, they need to explain in writing to the applicant why they are not returning it, within seven days of either the deadline for agreement passing or their decision not to let to the applicant, whichever is earlier.

Who keeps a forfeited holding deposit?

If the landlord uses an agent, there can be a debate over who keeps a holding deposit if it has been forfeited. On the one hand, the landlord will have paid for the referencing, but on the other, the letting agent will need to find another set of applicants.

The TFA doesn't say whether the landlord or the agent keep the holding deposit.

If there's nothing in the terms of business or the agency agreement specifically about the holding deposit, then the letting agent will have been holding it on behalf of the landlord under the laws of agency. This means they will need to forward it to the landlord.

However, if the agency agreement allows the agents to keep the holding deposit, they will be able to keep it themselves.

What happens to the holding deposit if the tenancy goes ahead?

If the tenancy goes ahead, the holding deposit can only be put towards either the first payment of rent or the tenancy deposit if the person who paid the deposit gives their consent.

With the RRA banning rent payments before the tenancy agreement is entered into, you can choose for the holding deposit to be put towards the first payment of rent once the tenancy is signed, so long as consent is given.

Letting agents and online letting platforms should ask for consent as standard, but if you're doing it yourself, make sure you do get consent. If they don't consent to it, they'll be able to recover the holding deposit from the First-tier Tribunal.

Here's an example of the sort of wording you could ask them to agree to:

I agree that if we enter into a tenancy agreement in respect of [address], the landlord may credit against the rent payable under the tenancy agreement the entire holding deposit of [£x] which I am paying to reserve the property.

Common mistakes with holding deposits

Here are common mistakes that agents and landlords make with holding deposits:

- The holding deposit is referred to as a "non-refundable fee".
- The property isn't taken off the market after a holding deposit has been accepted by the landlord or agent.
- The agents or landlord takes multiple deposits from different applicants for the same property.
- The applicants don't receive a draft tenancy agreement.

- The agents or landlord don't return the deposit when an applicant fails referencing. They should only keep the deposit when the applicant gives false or inaccurate information or fails a Right to Rent check.

Penalties for breaching the holding deposit rules

If the landlord or letting agent breaks the rules in the TFA, they can receive a civil penalty up to £5,000 for a first breach, and £30,000 for any subsequent breach in the following five years. Any subsequent breach is also a criminal offence.

A tenant can also complain to the local authority or the First-tier Tribunal and ask for the return of the holding deposit.

The landlord or letting agents will have a defence if the reason why they decided that the tenant didn't have the right to rent was the result of incorrect information provided by the Home Office.

3. Tenancy agreements

In this section, we go through the different types of tenancies.

Types of tenancy agreement

Abolition of assured shorthold tenancies

Assured shorthold tenancies (ASTs) were the default tenancy for individuals in England from 1997 until 30 April 2026.

All ASTs in place on 1 May 2026 automatically converted into assured periodic tenancies on that day, unless a valid section

21 notice had been served beforehand. (See Appendix 4 for more information.)

Landlords and letting agents must no longer offer ASTs to new tenants, not least because purporting to let for a fixed term is subject to a civil penalty of up to £7,000 for a first breach.

Assured periodic tenancies

Section 1 of the RRA amended the Housing Act 1988 to insert the new section 4A assured tenancy, known as an assured periodic tenancy or APT.

As explained in Chapter 2, this is now the default tenancy for tenants who are individuals (i.e. not a limited company), the property is the only or principal home of the tenant or at least one of the joint tenants, it is not a licence to occupy and is not a high or low rent tenancy.

All APTs are periodic rolling tenancies, without an end date. Any clause in agreement for an APT that tries to turn it into a fixed-term tenancy is null and void, and the local housing authority has the right to impose a civil penalty of up to £7,000 for a first breach if a landlord or an agent "purports to let for a fixed term".

The RRA bans clauses in new tenancy agreements which provide for rent to be paid at intervals of more than one calendar month, or in advance, e.g. six-monthly rent payments.

The RRA also introduced a new obligation into the HA 1988 to require landlords to provide a written statement of the terms of the tenancy before it is entered into. It makes sense to do this in a formal tenancy agreement which both parties sign, although it can be in a stand-alone document. I explain this in detail below.

Non-Housing Act tenancy agreements

Non-Housing Act (NHA) tenancy agreements are not regulated by the Housing Act 1988, the Renters' Rights Act 2025 or the Tenant Fees Act 2019. Instead, they operate under the common law, with the terms of the contract governing the relationship between the landlord and tenant.

For instance, they can be for a fixed-term period and rent review clauses are still valid. It is also possible to require rent to be paid in advance. NHA tenancies are also not subject to the rules regarding tenancy deposits, and landlords can charge fees for setting up and renewing the tenancy.

A landlord may terminate with a notice to quit in writing and is not required to use the process under section 8 HA88.

However, section 5 of the Protection from Eviction Act 1977 does apply, which means the landlord must give at least four weeks' notice (or a full rental period if longer) in writing if they wish to end the tenancy.

Joint tenants

If you rent to more than one adult in a household, the tenancy agreement should list each of the adults in the household as tenants. A household means every sort of couple and blended or extended family.

When two or more tenants sign the same tenancy agreement, regardless of whether they are in the same household, they will be "joint tenants" and share the same responsibilities to pay the rent and look after the property as if they were one person.

Landlords or agents can ask the tenants to choose a lead tenant to liaise with them. The deposit certificate will name the lead tenant.

Joint and several liability

Tenancy agreements will usually include a clause that spells out that joint tenants have "joint and several liability". This means that a couple or two sharers are both individually responsible (100%) and jointly responsible (50:50) for the rent. The landlord can choose who they pursue for the rent.

Notices to quit

Any one of the joint tenants can serve a notice to quit, which will bring the tenancy to an end for all.

However, if one joint tenant does serve a notice to quit, the landlord cannot agree to waive some of the notice period unless all of the tenants agree.

HMOs

There is no legal reason why sharers in an HMO cannot be joint tenants. However, for practical purposes, a joint tenancy for an HMO is more common when the sharers know each other and move in and out at the same time, for instance, students.

If the tenants don't know each other, moving in and out at different times, landlords tend to choose "room-only" tenancy agreements where a tenant or a couple rent a room and aren't joint tenants with the other people who live in the HMO.

Consequently, they won't be jointly and severally liable for the rent of the other people who rent rooms in the house; they are just responsible for their own rent and any damage they cause to their room.

Permitted occupiers

A permitted occupier is not a tenant but is someone who the landlord has agreed may live at the property with another tenant or tenants.

As they're not a tenant, they have no legal rights under the tenancy agreement and are not responsible for paying bills. If the tenancy comes to an end, the permitted occupier must move out as well and cannot stay in the property unless the landlord agrees to enter into a new tenancy agreement with them.

A common example of a permitted occupier is an adult child who is financially dependent on one or more parents who is a tenant. It could also be a partner who stays regularly at the property, but whose main home is elsewhere.

Landlords should make sure that their tenancy agreements have a clause that prevents anyone from living at the property without the written permission of the landlord, and not to sub-let the property. Even though they're not a tenant, a landlord still has a legal obligation to undertake a Right to Rent check on them before agreeing for someone to be a permitted occupier.

For the purposes of HMO licensing, permitted occupiers must be counted towards the total number of occupants, as the status of "occupant" under the Housing Act 2004 isn't determined by whether they have a formal tenancy or pay rent; it's solely based on whether they live there.

Written statement of terms

As mentioned in Chapter 2 the RRA introduced a strict legal duty for landlords to provide tenants with a written statement of terms before the tenancy is entered into. The local authority may impose a civil penalty of up to £7,000 if a landlord fails to do this.

This means you cannot have an informal, oral arrangement with tenants, and must give them a document which sets out the terms of the tenancy before tenants commit to renting a property. The document can either be a stand-alone document or included in the tenancy agreement.

The full requirements are set out in the *Written Statement etc Regulations*,[4] which include the following:

- The names of the parties.
- An address for service for the landlord.
- The date the tenancy starts.
- The rent: when payable and that any increase must be pursuant to a notice proposing a new rent in accordance with section 13 of the Housing Act 1988.
- List of any bills included in the rent.
- Details of any bills not included in the rent, for which

4. The Assured Tenancies (Private Rented Sector) (Written Statement of Terms etc and Information Sheet) (England) Regulations 2026.

the tenant must pay the landlord and not the service provider.

- The amount of tenancy deposit.
- The minimum notice period the tenant must give to serve a notice to quit to terminate the tenancy.
- Security of tenure: a statement explaining the landlord can only bring an end to the tenancy by obtaining an order of the court for possession of the property and the execution of the order, after having first served a notice under section 8 of the Housing Act 1988 relying on a valid ground.
- The landlord's obligation to ensure the property is fit for human habitation.
- The landlord's obligation to keep the property in repair under section 11 Landlord and Tenant Act 1985.
- The safety obligations regarding electrical installations and gas fittings and flues.
- Tenants' rights to a pet under section 16A of the Housing Act 1988.
- Tenants' rights under section 190 Equality Act 2010 to apply to make improvements for a disabled person.

Clauses for tenancy agreements

Here are examples of popular clauses for inclusion in an assured periodic tenancy agreement.

Service of documents by email

It will make your life a lot easier if you can serve documents by email. If the agreement doesn't already allow this, add a clause to an addendum authorising the parties to serve notices by email and specifying each party's email address. For instance, by including this clause, you will be able to send Gas Safety Certificates and the prescribed information for the tenancy deposit registration by email.

Don't forget to let the tenants know if you change your email address.

Fireplace use

If you have a blocked-up fireplace, include a clause that prohibits the tenants from trying to use the fireplace or burn any substance in the fireplace. Do also point this out to applicants during the viewing and when the tenants move in.

On the other hand, if the fireplace is in working order and you are happy for them to use it, you could mention this as an additional clause and say they will need to give access to a chimney sweep once a year.

Rent review clause

These were popular before the RRA came into force. However, as rent review clauses are no longer enforceable, you should not include one in an APT. Instead, you must use the section 13 process to increase rent and the written statement of terms must refer to this.

However, it is still possible to use rent review clauses in non-Housing Act tenancy agreements such as high rent tenancies.

Section 48 Landlord and Tenant Act 1987 notice

This is the notice that gives the tenants an address for them to serve notices on their landlords and applies to both APTs and non-Housing Act tenancies. The address must be included in the written statement of terms for APTs.

Landlords who use letting agents tend to use the address of their letting agents.

If you self-manage and live outside of England and Wales or do not wish to use your own address, you'll need to provide an address in England and Wales for the service of notices. It can be the address of anyone, but you will need to make sure they will forward notices promptly to you. For that reason, landlords who cannot or do not wish to use their own address often use the address of their solicitor or accountant.

Rent payment date

The rent payment date must be included in the written statement of terms for an APT.

Section 8 of the RRA amended the Housing Act 1988 to the effect that for APTs entered into after 1 May 2026, rent cannot be due before the first day of a rent period. There is an exception for the initial rent, which can be due in the period between signing the agreement and the start of the tenancy.

Consequently, the rent payment date is usually the first day of a rent period. For instance, if the tenancy starts on 15 January, the rent will be due on the 15th of every month.

Sometimes either the landlord or the tenant may wish to change the rent payment date at the start of the tenancy. However, as the RRA prohibits rent periods that are longer than one calendar month, you cannot have a long first rent period of one calendar month plus the number of additional days.

Instead, if you wish to move the rent payment day, you will need to have a short initial rent period to bring you to the desired rent payment date, and then move on to a monthly rent payment from there.

4. Tenancy deposits and deposit alternatives

It's usual for a landlord to ask the tenant to pay a tenancy deposit or take out a deposit alternative before they move into the property. A tenancy deposit gives the landlord some financial security against unpaid rent, damage or cleaning at the end of the tenancy.

Section 212 of the Housing Act 2004 requires landlords to safeguard tenancy deposits paid in connection with APTs in an authorised tenancy deposit scheme. At the time of print these are the Deposit Protection Service, MyDeposits and the Tenancy Deposit Scheme.

As well as being a means of protecting the tenant's deposit, the relevant scheme may also help resolve any disputes that arise at the end of the tenancy over deductions that the landlord would like to make. This is in addition to the parties' right to go to court.

Landlords must also register a deposit in their chosen scheme and serve on the tenant a signed copy of the scheme's prescribed information within 30 days of receiving the deposit.

Under the Tenant Fees Act 2019, the maximum deposit that a landlord can take from tenants is five weeks' rent, assuming the annual rent is under £50,000. If the annual rent is £50,000 or more, landlords may ask for a tenancy deposit of up to six weeks' rent. High rent tenancies (where the rent is over

£100,000 per year) are not covered by the TFA, so there is no legal cap on their deposit.

A landlord may seek deductions from the deposit where the tenant owes rent arrears, has damaged or lost items, or fails to return the property in the same condition as when they first let it, subject to usual wear and tear.

There are two different types of deposit protection for tenants: custodial and insurance, which all three deposit schemes offer. Letting agents are often keen to promote a "deposit alternative" or a "deposit replacement scheme", the details of which I provide below for completeness.

Custodial protection

With custodial protection, the landlord or agent forwards the deposit to one of the authorised tenancy deposit scheme providers, who keeps it in a secure bank account until the end of the tenancy. The scheme does this for free.

If you use letting agents for a tenant find and you're going to be managing the property yourself, ask for the deposit to be held in a custodial account in your own name. Otherwise, you will need to deal with the letting agent at the end of the tenancy to return the deposit to the tenant.

You can also ask the agent to send the deposit to you after you've shown proof that you have insurance with one of the authorised deposit schemes.

Insured protection

With an insured deposit, the landlord or letting agent holds the deposit and any interest that accrues and pays a fee to the scheme to insure it. The landlord or letting agent can keep the deposit, and any interest on the deposit, until the tenancy ends. The insurance covers the situation where the landlord or agent does not repay the balance of the deposit as required.

At the time of writing, the cost to landlords for an insured deposit over £500 for all three deposit schemes is a one-off payment that's under £30.

The insured scheme is popular with letting agents as they can charge the fees to the landlord and keep the interest in their bank accounts. Also, fees for letting agents are lower than the fees for landlords.

If a letting agent places the deposit in an insured scheme, the landlord won't be able to deal directly with the scheme administrators as per a custodial scheme.

Some letting agents charge a separate annual fee for holding the deposit in an insured scheme or include it in a monthly "compliance fee", even though the deposit schemes don't make further charges.

If the agent isn't providing full management services to the landlord, they may charge the landlord for dealing with the tenants if there's a dispute.

Service of prescribed information

Section 213 of the Housing Act 2004 requires the landlord or agent to provide the tenant with the prescribed information about the tenancy deposit and to anyone who paid the deposit on the tenant's behalf within 30 days of receiving the deposit. This includes all details required by the Housing (Tenancy Deposits) (Prescribed Information) Order 2007, together with the deposit protection scheme's official leaflet or explanatory notes.

Before the RRA abolished section 21, it was a requirement for a landlord to comply with these rules or return the deposit if they wished to enforce a section 21 notice.

The rules are different in the RRA for section 8 evictions. Landlords who don't protect the deposit within 30 days can protect the deposit late and still serve a notice for possession, provided they do protect the tenancy deposit or return it before they serve the notice.

Also, Grounds 7A (serious anti-social behaviour) and 14 (nuisance or criminal behaviour) are exempt from the deposit protection requirements, which means that landlords can apply for an order for possession using these grounds even if they have failed to protect or return the deposit.

TIP

Make sure you save in your electronic files a copy of the signed deposit protection certificate and details when the prescribed information was served, so it's easy to find in the future without hunting through emails!

I upload a copy to my online password-protected property manual for tenants.

Alternatives to deposits

As an alternative to a traditional deposit, there are "no deposit schemes" or "deposit replacement schemes" which provide landlords with a guarantee against financial loss or damage caused by tenants under their tenancy agreement.

Many letting agents promote these schemes to tenants and landlords. The agents typically receive a referral fee and don't have to handle the deposit as the tenant contacts the provider themselves.

However, landlords and agents must offer tenants the alternative of a traditional tenancy deposit. There's no obligation for a landlord to accept deposit alternatives, either.

I insist on a traditional tenant deposit as I like to keep it simple with tenants who pay a cash deposit upfront.

EXAMPLE: ZERO DEPOSIT

The tenant pays a fee of one month's rent plus a set-up fee of £59.99, followed by an annual fee of £17.50. These fees are not returnable to the tenant, even if they leave without causing any damage or being behind on the rent.

The Dispute Service (the same organisation as the Tenancy Deposit Scheme) assesses disputes about how much should be paid to the landlord at the end of the tenancy. If they conclude that the tenant needs to pay a certain amount, the tenant will need to pay this to the landlord, as Zero Deposit doesn't insure the tenant: it insures the landlord.

If the tenant doesn't pay the landlord what is due, Zero Deposit will pay it on their behalf and use a debt collection agency to collect it from the tenant, plus costs.

5. Guarantors

Landlords may ask for an applicant to provide a guarantor where they have concerns about the tenant's ability or willingness to pay the rent. This may be because the applicant is self-employed, has a poor credit history, a limited rental history (for instance, first-time renters and students) or irregular income.

Other landlords ask all tenants to provide a guarantor, even if the tenants meet the affordability criteria.

What is a guarantor liable for?

A guarantor is legally obliged to step in and pay on the tenant's behalf if the tenant doesn't pay the rent. If the guarantor doesn't pay, the landlord can apply for a county court judgment (CCJ) against both the tenant and the guarantor.

The guarantor only guarantees the rent that is stipulated in the deed of guarantee. If the rent increases, the landlord will need to arrange for the guarantor to sign another deed of guarantee with the higher rent.

It is possible for guarantors of joint tenants in HMOs to restrict their liability to paying the portion of rent payable by the tenant whose rent they are guaranteeing. This is called a "limited guarantee".

For assured periodic tenancies, the RRA specifically states that a guarantor cannot be held liable for rent payable after tenant's death. (Note that this does not apply to non-Housing Act tenancies, where liability depends on the specific wording of the deed of guarantee.)

Requirements for a guarantor

Guarantors should have an income at least four times the rent to ensure they can comfortably pay for their own living costs on top of the tenant's rent. (Some rent guarantee insurance providers will accept less than this).

It is preferable to have someone who is a homeowner in the UK.

Carry out the same credit checks and referencing on a guarantor as you would do with a tenant. Otherwise, the guarantee may be worthless.

Documentation

The landlord or agent must provide the guarantor with a copy of the tenancy agreement before they sign the guarantee, and send it to the guarantor, not via the tenant, to make sure that it is actually being signed by the guarantor.

The guarantee document itself is a deed, which needs to be signed and witnessed as a deed.

Professional guarantors

Professional guarantor services are designed for tenants who don't pass credit referencing, and can't provide a personal guarantor.

With the Renters' Rights Act ban on requesting more than one month's rent in advance, they are being heavily promoted as a risk mitigation solution.

The tenant pays a non-refundable fee to a company which then guarantees the rent to the landlord, typically covering arrears, property damage and eviction costs up to an agreed cap.

Fees are usually a percentage of the annual rent, in the region of 5–8%, and the tenant gets nothing back, regardless of whether they paid every penny on time.

If the guarantor has to pay out, the tenant remains liable for the debt.

This is an unregulated sector. Professional guarantors function much like insurance but are structured as guarantee deeds rather than insurance policies, which means they fall outside FCA regulation.

A professional guarantor is not equivalent to a personal guarantor. Treat it as one layer of risk management, not a complete solution.

This brings us to the end of the chapter on setting up a tenancy. The final chapter in Part II explains how to check in tenants.

CHAPTER 10

HOW TO CHECK IN TENANTS

Checking in tenants is a key "customer touchpoint" where they will get a feel for how you value them and the level of service they are likely to receive from you or your letting agents. It's important to think about how to make it a positive experience for the tenants at a time when they may be feeling anxious, and it helps to set the tone for the rest of the tenancy.

This chapter sets out what to do when tenants move in, including a list of the tenancy documents you need to serve, tips for check-in, and a summary checklist that recaps the key points on one page.

1. Check-in inventory

Although it's not a legal requirement, it's good practice for landlords to arrange for a professional inventory to be undertaken shortly before new tenants move in, and to provide a copy of the Inventory Report for the tenants.

A professional inventory report will have detailed date-stamped photos and written descriptions of the condition of every part of the property, inside and out. It will also include the meter readings and confirmation that the smoke alarms and carbon monoxide detectors have been tested.

Some landlords do an inventory themselves, either using software or taking photos and creating their own report. However, wearing my hat as a solicitor, my advice is to arrange for a professional inventory clerk to do this for you, as it will have a greater evidential value in the event of the dispute.

Providing a professional inventory is part of being a good landlord, as it is fair, protecting both the landlord and the tenant and setting the goal posts at the start of the tenancy. I believe it's a false economy not to pay for a qualified inventory clerk to do a thorough, professional inventory before tenants move in. An independent inventory also holds greater weight with tenants, who are more likely to see it as fair.

Ask the tenants to check the report carefully and to let the landlord or agent know whether they would like to make any corrections within seven days. If they don't, they will be deemed to accept it.

2. Service of tenancy documents

Landlords have a legal obligation to serve (or to arrange for their agents to serve) a number of documents on tenants before they move into the property.

Make sure you've handed over these documents before you check the tenants into the property:

1. Written statement of the terms of the tenancy. As this needs to be provided before an assured periodic tenancy is entered into, the easiest way to do it is to include it in the assured periodic tenancy agreement, which all parties sign.

2. A Gas Safety Certificate issued within the previous 12 months.
3. A satisfactory Electrical Installations Condition Report (EICR) issued within the previous five years.
4. An Energy Performance Certificate (EPC) that has a rating of E or better from within the previous ten years, which is due to increase to a C rating on 1 October 2030.
5. The prescribed information for the registration of the tenancy deposit, including the tenancy deposit scheme booklet, within 30 days of the tenant paying the deposit.

Note that before 1 May 2026, landlords were required to serve the latest *How to Rent* guide for tenants. However, following the abolition of assured shorthold tenancies and section 21 "no fault" evictions, this document was withdrawn.

Keep a record of the service of the above documents and ask the tenants to sign an acknowledgement that they've received them all when you check them in, if not before.

The acknowledgement can be as simple as stating "I confirm receipt of the following documents", with a list of the documents, the tenant's name, the date and room for the tenant's signature. A good time to do this is during the tenancy check-in.

3. The check-in

On the day that the new tenancy starts, the landlord, agent or a third party should meet the tenants at the property to hand them the keys, show them around and record that the relevant tenancy documents have been served on the tenants.

It's a nice touch to leave a "Welcome to your new home" card and a small gift.

Tips for showing tenants around

Walk around the property with the tenants, pointing out the following to them:

- Where the stopcock is, and how to turn it off.
- The consumer unit / fuse board.
- The meters for gas, electricity and water (often the water meter is outside on the pavement, under a small manhole).
- How the locks work on the doors – sometimes there is a knack to opening them.
- Which keys you are leaving.
- How to work the heating, and leave a printed manual.
- Test the CO and smoke alarms if the inventory wasn't carried out on the same day. If you have a heat sensor, test that as well.

Property manual

Landlords must provide instructions on how to use the boiler, heating system and any appliances.

A good way of doing this is to provide a property manual which includes practical things that they need to know about the property; for instance, where the stopcock is, links to the local council for parking permits and council tax, and the locations of the nearest hospital and Post Office.

This information can be provided as a hard copy document, or as a "live" document online, for instance, on a password-protected page on the landlord's website, in property management software or even in online folders such as Google Drive or One Drive.

Keys

The landlord or agent should hand over a set of keys for each tenant to retain. I add a spare set as well. Don't forget to keep copies of each of the keys in case you need access to the property in an emergency, or with the tenant's permission during the course of the tenancy agreement.

A professional inventory report will include a photo of the keys that are to be provided to the tenant.

Although it's not a legal obligation, it's good practice to change the locks to the external doors when tenants change, in case the previous tenant either didn't return all the keys or had spare copies of the keys cut.

Utilities and council tax

When a property is empty, the landlord is responsible for paying the utility bills and council tax, although some local authorities have an exemption for empty properties. Most water companies won't charge for water when the property is empty, unless there has been high usage, but you need to speak to them to tell them the property is empty.

Unless a property is an HMO, it's usual for the tenant to be responsible for paying electricity, gas, broadband, telephone line, water and council tax during the tenancy.

Meter readings

Landlords should ensure the utility companies and council know when new tenants move in so that the companies can prepare the final invoice with the correct meter readings and the tenants can take over responsibility for the bills.

To avoid any disputes later, someone should take readings of the meters for gas, electricity and water on the day the new tenants move in, ideally using a camera phone so each photo has a date. If you use a letting agent, do check with them that they (or the inventory company) are going to do this.

Meter readings will be included on the inventory check-in report, but not all landlords have a formal inventory.

I enter the meter readings onto the online accounts on the day the tenants move in. I don't provide the names of the tenants, as the tenants have a choice of utility supplier, but say that new tenants have moved in.

Council tax

For council tax, I register the new tenants on the council's portal and do give their names, as they will need to be registered for paying council tax and may need to be registered for a parking permit.

Establish an on-going communication channel

If the landlord uses agents to manage the property, the agent will establish a means of communicating between the property manager and the tenant so they can report repairs or ask questions. This may be via a portal or by email.

Self-managing landlords can also use a tenant management platform, which is useful if they use a virtual assistant to help with the management, or don't want to give out their personal mobile number. I keep it simple by creating a WhatsApp group for each property for communication, and have never had any trouble with this.

Arrangements for paying rent

Make sure the tenants know the arrangements for paying rent. The letting agents will do this if you are using them for a full management service, but they don't always pass on the landlord's bank details if the landlord will be taking over management after a tenant-find service.

If the tenants are to pay their rent direct to your bank account (or your limited company's bank account), make sure you give them the details and ask them to set up a standing order on the agreed rent payment date each month.

Book the first maintenance visit

It's good practice to arrange an informal maintenance visit for one or two weeks after they move in to check if any repairs are needed. This also enables you to check they are not sub-letting the property.

Ask them to make a note of any repairs that need doing so you can go through them when you visit.

4. Summary checklist for starting a new tenancy

Here's a summary of the steps that landlords or agents need to have done by the time new tenants have been fully checked in and the tenancy starts.

Before the tenancy agreement is signed

- Receive holding deposit from tenant and obtain permission to put it towards the rent after the agreement is entered into.
- Receive satisfactory reference and credit check for each tenant.
- Carry out Right to RENT checks for the tenants and any permitted occupiers aged 18 or over.
- Ensure the tenant receives the written statement of terms before the tenancy is entered into. This can be as a separate document or included in the tenancy agreement. (APTs only).
- Provide the guarantor with the tenancy agreement, and send the deed of guarantee for signature.
- Do not ask for or accept rent before all parties have entered into the tenancy agreement. (APTs only).

For the tenancy agreement

- Add details of any permitted occupiers.
- Don't use an old AST or a "home-brew" hybrid. Ensure the APT contains the information needed to comply with the requirements for the written statement of terms.

- Arrange for the guarantor to sign the deed of guarantee.
- Ensure the tenancy agreement is signed by all parties.

Between signing and when they move in

- Ask for the payment of the tenancy deposit. Register it with a deposit protection scheme and serve the prescribed information (a signed deposit protection certificate and the scheme booklet) to the tenants within 30 days of payment.
- Ask the tenants to pay the initial rent. The landlord cannot ask for more than one calendar month's rent – APTs only.
- Serve the safety documents on the tenants (a valid and up-to-date Gas Safety Certificate, EICR and full EPC) before they move in.
- Carry out a formal inventory of the condition of the property. Provide it to the tenants when it is completed, asking for comments within seven days.

Before handing over the keys

- Take meter readings for gas, electricity and water, and advise relevant utility companies of the meter readings.
- If the inventory clerk didn't do this, test the smoke and carbon monoxide alarms on the day the tenants move in, and make a record of this.
- Advise local authority that there is a new tenant for the purposes of council tax.

- Provide a property manual with instructions on how to use appliances.
- Give the tenants a set of keys for each tenant, and an optional spare set.
- Provide the tenants with bank details for the payment of rent, and ask them to set up a standing order.
- Ask each tenant to sign a confirmation that they have been served the tenancy documentation.
- Check in the tenant.

After the start of the tenancy

- Arrange your first maintenance / inspection visit for a few weeks' time, after the tenants have settled in.
- Make sure you save in your electronic files a copy of the signed deposit protection certificate and details when the prescribed information was served.

That brings us to the end of Part II on what landlords need to do before the tenancy starts, and we now move on to Part III, which discusses what to do during the tenancy.

PART III

DURING THE TENANCY

CHAPTER 11

PROPERTY MANAGEMENT

Once the tenants have moved in, someone needs to look after both them and the property and ensure compliance with the landlord's many legal obligations.

While many landlords prefer to use a letting agent for property management, a large proportion of landlords manage their portfolio themselves.

In this chapter, I provide detailed guidance both on how landlords can manage their own rental properties themselves and how they can use agents effectively for property management.

When I say "agents", I mean businesses which provide property management services to landlords, whether they're part of a letting agency, estate agency or a specialist property management company.

The first two sections deal with the management of single let properties, followed by a dedicated section on HMO management at the end.

When I refer to a single let, I mean letting to one household or to two sharers who are joint tenants but are not a couple or related. If there are three or more tenants from two or more households, it is an HMO.

1. Managing a single let property yourself

How many landlords self-manage?

According to the *2024 English Private Landlord Survey*, 82% of landlords manage their rental properties themselves, although as I mention in Chapter 1, this figure is probably overstated due to the sampling methodology.

Goodlord's *2025 State of the Lettings Industry Report*, on the other hand, estimates that 43% of landlords self-manage.[1]

On the assumption that the number is probably somewhere in between, it is clear that a significant proportion of landlords do not use a letting agent to manage their properties.

Do landlords need qualifications to self-manage?

There is no legal obligation on landlords to undergo training or accreditation before managing their own rental properties, unless the local authority requires it in a selective licensing area. The same is true of letting agents.

Landlords will need to register with the PRS Database and join the PRS Landlord Ombudsman, when launched, whether or not they use agents for property management.

Self-managing landlords do not need to join a letting agent redress scheme.

1. Goodlord, *2025 State of the Lettings Industry Report*, https://www.goodlord.com/state-of-the-lettings-industry-report-2025. The sample size was 1,350 landlords with an average portfolio size of 7.4 properties.

Is self-management right for you?

To successfully manage your own rental properties, you'll need to be organised, be good at keeping records and have effective communication skills.

If you're already a homeowner, you'll be used to arranging for your boiler to be serviced and carrying out repairs. It's very similar for landlords, who arrange for tradespersons to carry out repairs in their rental properties.

I've always managed my own properties. Research by OSB Group showed that tenants tend to be happier when the landlord manages the property themselves,[2] and happy tenants are the key to long-term success.

Self-managing is not for everyone. However, I believe that a landlord who genuinely cares about their properties and the people who live in them, and who has taken the time to learn about their legal obligations, is likely to do it better than an agent for whom it may be just another job.

What does self-management involve?

Property management starts after the tenants check in, although if the landlord found the tenants themselves, it's a continuation of what they have already been doing. If the landlord used agents to find the tenant, the agent hands over responsibility after the check-in and the completion of any inventory report.

---

2. OSB Group, *Research: A Future Tenant Standard,* https://landlordleaders.osb.co.uk/collaboration/tenant-research.

Communicating with tenants

A self-managing landlord (or someone working for them) is the point of contact for the tenant. I set up a WhatsApp group for each property with all the tenants and communicate with them that way.

Other landlords use property management software or an assistant who does the administration remotely, often called a "VA" or a virtual property assistant.

Collecting rent

The tenant pays the rent directly to the landlord, and the landlord is responsible for following up on any missed payments.

Increasing rent

The landlord will need to assess whether the rent has fallen behind the market, and if so, increase the rent.

As discussed in Chapter 14, it is mandatory to use the section 13 procedure to increase the rent for APTs, and any rent review clauses in old ASTs are no longer valid.

Keys

The landlord should keep a spare set of keys for the property in case of an emergency or to let in a tradesperson, provided the tenant agrees to this. However, a landlord should never let themselves in without the tenant's permission unless it's an emergency.

Repairs and maintenance

Inevitably, there will be repairs and maintenance to attend to, which the landlord will need to arrange an appropriate tradesperson to do, unless they do it themselves. I cover this in detail in Chapter 12.

This is in addition to arranging an annual Gas Safety Certificate and other relevant safety checks and assessments.

Inspections

I recommend inspecting the property at least twice a year, and even more frequently for HMOs, so you can check the condition of the property and see if there is anything untoward going on there. Some landlord insurance requires more frequent inspections.

See Chapter 13 for more details on inspections.

How to get organised

Letting property is highly regulated, and it's important for self-managing landlords to be organised. If you can't prove you have complied with a legal obligation, it's almost as if you didn't comply with it. This is even more important for landlords now that the RRA has introduced so many civil penalties for non-compliance.

Start as you mean to go on by setting up a system from the beginning, or turn over a new leaf now, if you haven't done it before.

Here are some tips to help you get organised:

Set up a filing system

Self-managing landlords need to store important documents safely and efficiently to find them easily, without having to search through years of emails.

Set up a cloud-based filing system (Google Drive, OneDrive, iCloud or similar). Cloud storage means you won't lose files if your laptop crashes and you can access them remotely.

Create a folder for each property with sub-folders for tenancy documents, documents served, safety certificates, risk assessments, insurance, mortgage and financing, and invoices. If you save or scan documents and file them in the relevant folder as soon as you receive them, you'll always be up to date.

Filing invoices electronically makes things easier for unincorporated landlords to upload into Making Tax Digital (MTD) approved accounting software.

Those landlords who prefer hard copies can print off documents and save them in a traditional filing cabinet. In any event, it is worth keeping back-up copies of the key documents electronically in case there's a fire and you lose your hard copy documents.

Ultimately it doesn't matter how you set up your filing system; the important thing is that you set it up so you can easily find things in the future.

Set calendar reminders

Set up calendar reminders, or reminders in your property management software, for two months before and then two days before the renewal dates of the Gas Safety Certificate (annual), landlord insurance (annual), EICR (every five years) and EPC (every ten years, although it currently doesn't need renewing until the next tenancy).

When you renew a safety certificate, put an updated renewal date into your calendar or software. Also add in reminders if a tenant has a time-limited right to rent. Finally, put another reminder in your calendar for when you need to get in touch with the tenants to arrange inspections.

Landlord journal

As well as filing all the documents, you need to keep records of communications with your tenants, particularly those relating to repairs, access, inspections, rent increases and changes to the tenancy agreement.

This can be as simple as a Word document per property into which you cut and paste screen shots of important messages, and add notes of conversations. Some property management software platforms enable you to do this as well.

PRS Database and Ombudsman

Once launched, you will need to have active landlord and property entries on the PRS Database and membership of the PRS Landlord Ombudsman. See Chapter 2 for more details.

Using virtual assistants

Property management virtual assistants or VAs have become popular with landlords with larger portfolios who don't want to do the day-to-day management of their portfolios themselves, but equally don't want to use a letting agent.

VAs are remote assistants (not AI) who provide a wide range of administrative and business support. This includes the tasks letting agents do where someone doesn't need to be physically present. The particular tasks vary but can include handling repair requests, dealing with tenant onboarding and producing management information.

VAs enable landlords to benefit from economies of scale as their portfolio expands, because adding an extra property doesn't have a big impact on the monthly cost of a VA. With an agent, on the other hand, the cost will go up by 10–20% of the gross rent, depending on the fee.

Having a VA isn't a totally hands-off experience for a landlord, as they still require management, particularly if the VA is based abroad. Someone will still need to be available to visit the properties for inspections and repairs.

Nevertheless, VAs are a cost-effective way for portfolio landlords to lighten the load of self-management.

Checklist for self-managing landlords

In summary, here are the key things that landlords need to do to manage their own rental properties successfully:

- Set up a filing system to save all important documents and keep it updated.
- For unincorporated landlords, upload and reconcile invoices and receipts to MTD-approved accounting software as you go along (or provide them to your accountant to do so on your behalf).
- Set up reminders for when certificates need renewing

and inspections are due in your calendar or property management software.

- For single lets, arrange inspections for within one month of the tenants moving in, and then every six months or so afterwards (more if required by your landlord insurance or licence).
- Inspections of HMOs need to be more frequent, depending on the risk. A minimum of every three months is a good rule of thumb.
- Monitor rent payments systematically and send reminders promptly if tenants miss a rent payment.
- Keep records of communications with tenants, for instance, using a landlord journal or software
- Build up a list of trusted tradespersons you can call on to carry out repairs. Pay them promptly and get a reputation for being a good landlord to work with.
- Register and comply with the requirements for the PRS Database and the PRS Landlord Ombudsman, once they are launched.

2. Single let management by agents

In this section, the focus is on using agents to manage single let properties, to ensure they provide a good service for you and your tenants. I deal with the management of HMOs in the next section.

Why landlords can't "let and forget"

It can be very tempting to leave the agent to get on with the management of rental properties, assuming they are doing it correctly, and trusting them to handle the inevitable problems the right way. People assume that no news is good news. But it's not. It's just no news.

Whilst there are many competent agents who are excellent at managing property, there are many who are not. Some agencies have a high turnover of staff, which means there's a lack of continuity.

With the complexity introduced by the Renters' Rights Act, choosing agents with qualified staff is more important than ever. See Chapter 4 for more details.

Property managers typically only visit rental properties once a year, and your rental property may be just another address in a list of addresses to tick off the list. They are unlikely to know the property well or be aware what refurbishment work has been carried out, particularly if there has been a turnover of property managers. Sometimes agents arrange repairs without finding the root cause of the problem.

How to check agents are doing a good job

Here are some examples of how landlords can check that their agents are looking after the property and the tenants who are living in the property:

Ask for repair logs

Ask for the agent to provide regular summaries of repairs logged by the tenants and action taken, even if it's a minor repair. Small problems may be symptoms of something bigger, e.g. the lights not working in the bathroom might mean there is a leak in the roof or a problem with the extractor fan. This may give you early warning of bigger issues.

Insist on follow-up visits

Insist there is a follow-up visit a month later if damp and mould is present during an inspection. This is to see if the measures the agents recommended to the tenants have worked, or whether further intervention is needed.

Attend inspections yourself

Accompany the agent on at least one inspection a year. This will enable you to see the condition of the property yourself and plan for longer-term repairs. You can also meet the tenants and ask them yourself whether they're happy with the service, and whether they think any repairs are needed.

What if you're unhappy with the service?

If you're unhappy with the service, document it, and if you fail to resolve the matter informally, make a formal complaint to the agent in accordance with their complaints procedure.

The letter should set out why you're unhappy and what the agent needs to do to rectify the problem, referring to any breaches of the agency agreement.

If you're unhappy with the response or if they don't respond, you can escalate it to their redress scheme.[3] Reserve your right to terminate the agreement on the grounds of their breach of contract.

3. Letting agents have a legal obligation to join a redress scheme, which is an independent service that resolves complaints between letting agents and their customers.

Keep copies of your data and documentation

If you use agents, you should keep copies of your data and documentation, so you know what's going on. This also means that if you ever decide to leave the agent, you'll have the historical documents for each tenancy. Some agents supply documents on a portal, but others only supply them if the landlord asks.

If the agent says they can't provide this to the landlord, they are legally incorrect. The agent works on behalf of the landlord. So long as the landlord registers online with the ICO and has a Data Protection Notice, there is no legal reason the agent cannot provide the information to the landlord.

Landlords should ask their agents to provide them with the following for each tenancy as a matter of course on an on-going basis, even if they have no plans to self-manage:

- The full names and contact details of every tenant.
- Copies of tenancy agreements and any amendments.
- Details of rent increases including copies of any section 13 notices and what proof they have of the market rent.
- Copies of the check-in inventories and any inspection reports.
- Copies of the Gas Safety Certificates, EICRs and EPCs.
- Details of repairs per property, including any guarantees. Ask for copies of the original invoices so there is full transparency over which contractor did the work.
- Deposit information, but bear in mind you have more control if the deposits are in a custodial or insured account in your name.

- Copies of any licences.
- Copies of references and credit checks for all tenants, permitted occupiers and sub-tenants. (No need to ask for those of unsuccessful applicants.)

3. HMO management

In this section, I discuss the management of rental properties in which three or more people live, who aren't from the same household, and who share facilities such as kitchens and bathrooms. These are HMOs, which fall under section 254 Housing Act 2004.[4]

Appointing a suitable HMO manager

If you're not able to manage your HMO yourself, you'll need to appoint someone else to manage it on your behalf and be responsible for complying with the HMO Management Regulations, which I cover in the next section.[5]

Many letting agents provide specialist HMO property managers. However, it is important that the manager has experience in managing HMOs and has had adequate training, so they understand the many legal obligations on HMO landlords.

When choosing a property manager, ask what percentage of the properties they manage are HMOs, and quiz them about their approach to managing HMOs, and how they think it

4. Note that the management of section 257 HMOs (some converted blocks of flats) is subject to similar regulations, but is outside the scope of this book.
5. The Management of Houses in Multiple Occupation (England) Regulations 2006.

differs from managing single lets. If they can't spell it out for you, go elsewhere.

Tenant safety is clearly key for HMO management. But also, good landlords choose managers who genuinely care about looking after the property and providing a good service for tenants. It's not just what the manager does, but how they go about it. They need to have the right customer-focused attitude, rather than seeing it all as one giant "to do" list.

HMO Management Regulations

Managing an HMO is a different proposition from managing a property which is let to a family or a couple, due to the practicalities of having to manage so many different households. HMOs are also subject to considerably more onerous regulation than properties let to a single household or two sharers, in the form of the HMO Management Regulations.

Under the HMO Management Regulations, the HMO manager has a legal duty to comply with the following, so far as is reasonable when considering the age, character and "prospective life of the house", as well as its location:

Contact details

The HMO manager must place a notice in a prominent position in the HMO of their name, address and a telephone contact number.

It's a good idea for these details to be laminated and put on a notice board in the common parts of the HMO.

Fire safety

The manager must keep in good repair the fire exits, fire-fighting equipment and alarms. They must also check the means of escape regularly to make sure there are no hazards in the way, such as bikes or appliances blocking the exit.

General safety

There are very wide obligations on the HMO manager to take "all such measures as are reasonably required to protect the occupiers of the HMO from injury" in relation to the design of the HMO, its "structural conditions" (including any roof, balcony and windows) and the number of occupiers.

Water supply

The manager must ensure the water supply and drains are maintained "in good, clean and working condition". This includes the water tanks for drinking water and any fittings such as pipes, cisterns, taps, baths, showers and toilets.

Gas and electricity

As for all rental properties, HMOs must have a Gas Safety Certificate each year and an EICR every five years.

The HMO manager must not "unreasonably cause" the gas or electricity supply to be cut off.

Common parts

The HMO manager must maintain the common parts so that they are in "good and clean decorative repair, in a safe working condition, and kept reasonably clear from obstruction". This includes all handrails and banisters, stair coverings, windows, light fittings, fixtures and fittings in the common parts.

Common parts also include any outbuildings, yards, forecourts, garden, boundary walls, fences and railings that belong to the HMO and are used by two or more households.

Any passageway and staircase leading to the HMO need to be kept "reasonably clean and free from refuse and litter". This might include the stairs leading up to an HMO flat in an apartment building.

Living accommodation

The room and any furniture supplied by the landlord must be clean when the occupier moves in. Also, the manager needs to maintain the "internal structure", which includes keeping fixtures, fittings or appliances in "good repair and in clean working order", and keep the windows and ventilation methods (e.g. extractor) in good repair.

However, the manager isn't obliged to carry out repairs to damage that the tenant has caused or any damage to the tenant's own possessions.

Disposal of rubbish

The manager needs to ensure there are enough bins for the property, and appropriate storage for the bins, considering the service provided by the local council, in accordance with any licence, and the Simpler Recycling rules which are due to start coming into effect in 2026.[6]

The manager should check periodically to see if the occupiers are putting out the correct bins for collection.

Proactive management

HMOs need proactive rather than reactive management. This means that HMO managers shouldn't just wait until a tenant reports a repair. They are liable straight away when a problem arises, even if they don't know about it.

HMO managers must inspect the property regularly and keep proper records to show that they are managing the HMO properly. The frequency of the inspections will vary according to the risk involved.

I cover HMO inspections in Chapter 13.

Self-managing HMOs

Managing an HMO is significantly harder than managing a single let, especially if the HMO requires a licence. Due to these complexities, if you manage your own HMO, you should have specific training on HMO management.

Most local authorities will give landlords a discount on the licensing fees if the landlord has accreditation from an

6. Department for Environment, Food and Rural Affairs, *Simpler Recycling: Household Recycling in England*. Guidance (2025), https://www.gov.uk/guidance/simpler-recycling-household-recycling-in-england.

approved scheme, and some (for instance, Portsmouth) make accreditation a condition for receiving a five-year licence.

Fit and proper persons

For licensed HMOs, the licence-holder and manager both need to be a "fit and proper person", and the council must be satisfied the licence-holder and manager have the character and record to run the HMO lawfully.

Under section 66 Housing Act 2004, the local authority must consider whether the applicant, or anyone closely involved with them, has unspent convictions for violence, drugs, sexual offences, fraud or dishonesty, serious breaches of housing or landlord and tenant law, past revocations or refusals of HMO licences, or a current banning order.

Additionally, the applicant must not have "practised unlawful discrimination on grounds of sex, colour, race, ethnic or national origins or disability in, the carrying on of any business".

The local authority must also consider whether they are sufficiently competent and whether the "proposed management structures and funding" are suitable. The council will also ask for evidence of competence and adequate management arrangements, cross-checking its own enforcement files and the records of other authorities.

If the council decides that an applicant is not a fit and proper person, the landlord should nominate a different manager or agent who is fit and proper to hold the licence.

In the next chapter, I go through how to handle common issues that arise during a tenancy.

CHAPTER 12

COMMON ISSUES DURING A TENANCY

In this chapter, we get into the nuts and bolts of property management and tenant management: how to handle common issues that arise during a tenancy.

1. Repairs and maintenance

Keeping a rental property in good repair is not only a legal obligation for landlords, but it also makes good business sense. Houses and flats are expensive assets which need looking after. A well-maintained property will preserve its value and be a nice home for your tenants.

In this section, I share tips on how to keep on top of repairs and maintenance.

Proactive preventative maintenance

The key to cost-effective maintenance is fixing things before they get worse. A broken down-pipe won't fix itself, and the water damage it causes will cost far more than replacing the damaged section. It's best to nip problems in the bud through proactive maintenance, whether spotted in inspections or reported by tenants.

A good example is having the gas engineer service the boiler during the annual gas safety check. The modest additional cost extends the boiler's life and reduces breakdowns. Another is clearing gutters annually if there are nearby trees. Few tenants will own a long ladder, so waiting for them to do it is unrealistic.

Arranging repairs

If you manage your own property, you can save money by doing minor repairs yourself, so long as you know what you're doing. If your gas engineer also does plumbing, batch non-urgent plumbing jobs with the annual gas safety visit to save call-out charges.

When organising repairs, I put the tradesperson in touch with the tenant to arrange a time for them to come and do the repair.

Sometimes it can be difficult if the tenants are never home in the day, so with the permission of the tenant, the agent or the landlord can let the tradesperson into the property to carry out the repair and stay there until the repair is completed.

As discussed in Chapter 3, section 11 of the Landlord and Tenant Act 1985 gives landlords an implied right to enter the property to carry out repairs with 24 hours' notice. However, this is subject to the tenant's right of quiet enjoyment, which means that tenants have the right to refuse access.

This is one of the many reasons why it's important to have a good relationship with tenants, and to try to see things from their perspective. I always give considerably more than 24 hours' notice, and work around their schedule. Many of the tenants are even happy for me to let myself in to supervise the repairs while they are at work.

There's a shortage of plumbers, electricians, builders and other trades in the UK, so it can be very difficult for both letting agents and landlords to find tradespersons to carry out maintenance and repairs. This is particularly true for small jobs like replacing a broken extractor fan.

Build good relationships with tradespersons by being reliable, not saying something is urgent unless it is and paying invoices promptly. Use local contractors for safety certification where possible. They're more likely to help loyal customers in an emergency.

Failing that, you can use online services such as Checkatrade, My Builder or A Trader to help you find reliable tradespersons.

Dealing with pests and vermin

Pests and vermin, especially rodents, can do a lot of damage to a property, as well as being very unpleasant for the tenants living there. Rats and mice are endemic in many cities, and fleas and bedbugs can be a big problem in furnished rental properties.

However, it's not always clear who is responsible for dealing with them, as the liability from a legal perspective depends on the cause of the infestation, and the cause isn't always obvious.

Landlord obligations

Section 9A of the Landlord and Tenant Act 1985 (LTA) requires landlords to ensure that the property is fit for human habitation when the tenant moves in, and to remain so throughout the tenancy.

This also includes keeping the property free from hazards such as pests where the pests are due to poor design, layout and construction, making it hard for the tenant to keep the property clean, which attracts pests. Landlords should ensure there are enough bins for the property and the number of people at the start of the tenancy.

Make sure the property is thoroughly clean before the tenants move in. A detailed professional inventory with photos will help prove the property was clean and that there were no signs of pest infestation at the start of the tenancy.

Tenant obligations

Tenants have responsibilities too, and the law recognises that a landlord shouldn't be held liable for a pest infestation caused by the tenant's own behaviour.

Under the LTA, a landlord isn't responsible if the unfitness is "wholly or mainly attributable" to the tenant's own breach of contract or failure to behave in a "tenant-like manner." If rubbish has been piling up because the tenant hasn't been putting the bins out for collection, and this has attracted rats or maggots, the tenant is at fault, not you.

Equally, you won't be liable if the tenant has refused to allow you or your contractors access to inspect the property's condition and carry out repairs.

If a pest problem is down to the tenant's behaviour, write to them formally and ask them to put it right. Follow up to make sure they do. You should still arrange for a professional pest control service to deal with the infestation, but you can charge the tenant for the cost if it's clearly their fault.

If, on the other hand, mice are getting in because of gaps in the mortar or another structural defect, that's your responsibility. You need to fix the defect and pay for pest control.

Where it's not clear whose fault it is, the pragmatic approach is to pay for pest control yourself as leaving an infestation untreated will only make it worse.

HMOs

As explained in Chapter 11, HMO landlords and managers have an additional layer of legal obligations to manage waste disposal in the HMO Management Regulations.

The regulations require managers to ensure there are enough appropriate bins for the HMO and make further arrangements if necessary. The regulations also require the landlord to ensure that the garden, yard, passageways, etc. are kept clean and free of refuse and litter. Some HMO landlords manage this by arranging for a cleaner to put the main bins out, if the tenants often forget to do it themselves. These measures will help reduce the risk of pests and vermin from rubbish.

Local authority action

If pests and vermin become a problem, the local authority can bring an action against the landlord, for instance, an abatement notice under the Environmental Protection Act 1990 for a statutory nuisance that is prejudicial to health, or an improvement or prohibition order under the Housing Act 2004.

2. Damp and mould

The tragic death of two-year-old Awaab Ishak in 2020 due to black mould in the flat his parents rented from a housing association underlined just how important it is for landlords to take damp and mould seriously.

As well as potentially being bad for physical health, damp and mould are often very distressing and can adversely affect mental health.

Managing damp and mould is one of the most difficult challenges as a landlord. This is because there's often more than one reason why a particular wall is damp, and it's usually not solely due to the "lifestyle" of the tenants.

What are landlords' legal responsibilities for damp and mould?

Landlords have a legal obligation to ensure that their rental properties are fit for tenants to live in and free from health hazards. Landlords are also responsible for maintaining the fabric of the building to remove external sources of moisture to reduce the risk of damp and mould.

From a legal perspective, damp and mould growth are a hazard under the HHSRS classification system, and serious damp and mould can lead to enforcement action by the local authorities.

According to the MHCLG's *Guidance on Damp and Mould,*[1] landlords must take damp and mould seriously, assess the

1. Ministry of Housing, Communities and Local Government, *Guidance: Understanding and Addressing the Health Risks of Damp and Mould in the Home:* https://www.gov.uk/government/publications/damp-and-mould-understand ing-and-addressing-the-health-risks-for-rented-housing-providers/under

underlying causes with urgency, take appropriate action and keep tenants informed. It's also important for landlords to "regularly inspect their properties, remedy deficiencies promptly and ensure that they have a regular programme of maintenance and management".

Landlords will also need to "take action" in relation to damp and mould under Awaab's Law when it comes into force, although the precise detail of what this will mean in practice for private landlords has not yet been confirmed by the Government.

The Decent Homes Standard will also require rental properties to be free of damp and mould when it comes into force in 2035. In the words of the 2026 *Policy Paper*: "This means landlords should address damp and mould when it is reported to them by their tenants as well as taking a proactive approach to prevention".[2]

What causes damp?

There are three key causes of damp: condensation, penetrating or water-ingress damp (including plumbing leaks and rain penetration) and rising damp.

Salts deposited by rising damp tend to suppress mould, and rising damp rarely affects walls above ground-floor level.

---

standing-and-addressing-the-health-risks-of-damp-and-mould-in-the-home--2.

2. Ministry of Housing, Communities and Local Government, *The New Decent Homes Standard: Policy Statement* (2026).

What causes condensation mould?

Condensation mould is a fungus that thrives in damp, dark conditions and can be highly damaging to health. The most common form is "black mould", but other fungi grow wherever surfaces remain wet from repeated condensation. Condensation occurs when warm, moist air meets a colder surface (typically an external wall or window), causing the moisture to condense.

Leaky pipes can also cause or exacerbate mould, as can rain entering through cracks or damaged roofs.

Mould often begins in the corners of rooms and ceilings, growing behind wardrobes and cupboards, and along the top of the skirting board where moisture collects. It lurks behind furniture that's up against an external wall in a bedroom.

It is common in kitchens and bathrooms without extractor fans, or which are not cleaned adequately. Smaller room sizes also contribute to the growth of mould from condensation because a smaller volume of air saturates more quickly when moisture is added, so the relative humidity rises faster, increasing condensation risk.

What should a landlord do if a tenant reports damp or mould?

If a tenant reports damp or mould, the landlord (and agent) should take it very seriously, investigate the causes promptly, determine whether remedial work needs to be carried out to tackle the underlying causes and keep the tenant informed. If you use a letting agent, make it clear that you expect them to notify you if the tenant reports damp and mould.

The MHCLG's *Guidance* states landlords must "treat tenants' reports of damp and mould with urgency" and "identify and address the underlying cause".[3]

There are a number of defects in the fabric of the building that can cause or contribute to damp and mould, and which are the landlord's responsibility to repair. For instance, leaking internal pipes, such as waste pipes, water pipes, and pipes to radiators, and leaks due to baths and showers that are not adequately sealed, e.g. missing grouting or silicone.

Other causes are missing roof tiles, faulty and/or blocked guttering or downpipes, cracks in walls and rotten window frames. Insufficient insulation and inadequate heating also exacerbate damp and mould.

How landlords can help reduce condensation mould

There are several things that landlords can do to prevent or at least reduce mould caused by condensation.

Firstly, investigate the causes of the condensation, taking advice from a suitably qualified expert if the cause is not obvious. There may be leaks or other sources of water that are adding to the problem of condensation.

Install extractor fans that are vented to the outside in kitchens and bathrooms. Sometimes mechanical ventilation is needed

3. Ministry of Housing, Communities and Local Government, *Understanding and Addressing the Health Risks of Damp and Mould in the Home* (15 August 2024), Guidance, https://www.gov.uk/government/publications/damp-and-mould-understanding-and-addressing-the-health-risks-for-rented-housing-providers/understanding-and-addressing-the-health-risks-of-damp-and-mould-in-the-home--2.

with the installation of a positive input ventilation (PIV) system in the loft to eliminate or significantly reduce condensation. If the radiators in the rooms with mould have only one panel, replacing them with large radiators with two panels can improve the heating in the rooms.

Often tenants don't understand that condensation can lead to mould. It's therefore important to explain how they need to improve ventilation and control moisture, and why they need to clean away mould to break the cycle.

Ask the tenants to alert the landlord or letting agent if the mould comes back, or if they notice any leaks, so that the landlord can investigate further.

It's a good idea to follow up with tenants by text, as sometimes they don't like to make additional reports.

Follow up with a visit about six weeks after carrying out any remedial work, to make sure that the damp and mould have not come back. Sometimes damp and mould will seem to disappear over the summer, only to come back with a vengeance when the weather turns cold.

Even if the mould seems to go, inspect the property again in six months' time, as often tenants are reluctant to report problems. November is a good time to inspect a property, as that is when mould usually starts to reappear.

What are tenants' responsibilities for controlling mould?

Tenants are required to act in a "tenant-like manner",[4] which includes taking reasonable steps to control mould.

Often tenants aren't aware of what they can do to keep on top of it. It's better to explain things in person than give them a leaflet that they might not read.

Here are some practical tips which landlords or their agents can go through with their tenants.

Heating

Adequate heating is important in reducing mould. By heating a room to at least 14°C, the coldest surfaces will stay above the dew-point to help prevent airborne moisture from condensing on walls and windows. Without that film of water, mould spores cannot germinate and grow.

Ventilation

However, heating alone cannot overcome very high moisture loads, which is why ventilation is so important. Landlords should install good quality extractor fans in the kitchen and the bathroom as standard to help remove moisture-laden air from the room.

Encourage tenants to turn the extractor fan on in the kitchen when cooking (if there is one), and to put on the fan in the bathroom when having a bath or shower. Afterwards, they

4. *Warren v Keen*, [1953] EWCA, Court of Appeal, https://vlex.co.uk/vid/warren-v-keen-792939905.

should open the window for at least ten minutes with the bathroom door closed so the moisture escapes and doesn't spread to the rest of the property.

Furniture placement

The space immediately behind a wardrobe, bed or curtains can become a stagnant, cold micro-climate, below the dew-point, where moisture can condense on the chilled paintwork. Leaving a 10 cm gap between the furniture and the wall allows warmer air to circulate so the wall surface stays above the dew-point.

Drying clothes

Drying clothes inside can drastically increase the amount of moisture inside the property that may condense on cold walls. In order to reduce the risk of this, ask tenants not to dry clothes in bedrooms or on radiators. If the tenant cannot dry clothes outside, the best choice is using an airer over the bath with the door shut, the window open and the heating on.

Tumble dryers generate a lot of moisture, so make sure any dryer in your property is either a condenser model or vented to the outside.

Condensation on windows

If condensation is a problem on windows, tenants should wipe away the condensation each day and open bedroom windows for at least ten minutes every morning. Condensation is more of an issue with single-glazed windows than double-glazed modern windows.

Cleaning and reporting

Tenants should keep a particular eye on the kitchen and bathroom, and clean mould away with anti-mould products.

Finally, it's important to explain to tenants why they should report any new leaks promptly and let the landlord or letting agent know if the mould comes back or if they are unsure what they need to do.

3. Sub-letting

What is sub-letting?

Sub-letting arises when a tenant sub-lets some or all of a property they rent from a landlord (called the superior landlord or the head landlord) to another person (the sub-tenant).

The tenant becomes the landlord of the sub-tenant, as an intermediate landlord in between the superior landlord and the sub-tenant. The tenant still remains responsible for complying with the terms of their tenancy agreement with the superior landlord, including paying the rent and behaving in a tenant-like manner.

Sub-letting is a very complex area for tenants and landlords to navigate and is full of risk.

SUB-LETTING SCENARIOS

A good long-term tenant is going away for a set period, and a friend wants to live there on a temporary basis (and it won't be their sole or primary home). Here it might make sense for a landlord to give consent for the tenant to sub-let the property or room to another person.

On the other hand, if they're not planning to come back, it would be better for the tenant to serve a notice to quit and begin a new direct tenancy with the new person.

The risks of sub-letting

Importantly, if a landlord authorises sub-letting and the sub-tenant has the exclusive use of the property, which is also their sole or primary residence, the sub-tenant will have the right to "quiet enjoyment". This means that the landlord and tenant will only be able to enter the accommodation with the sub-tenant's permission.

The rights of authorised sub-tenants

If the landlord has authorised the sub-letting, the sub-tenant will also have the usual rights of a tenant with an assured periodic tenancy, even though they are a sub-tenant. This creates risk for the landlord, as their tenant may not be able to recover possession from the sub-tenant.

Even if the landlord evicts the tenant, the sub-tenancy will still continue, as it is protected under section 18 of the Housing Act 1988. As a result, the landlord will become the direct landlord of the sub-tenant and will not be able to recover possession unless they have a valid ground under section 8 of the Housing Act 1988.

Unauthorised sub-letting

Unauthorised sub-letting carries additional risks as the landlord won't have been able to check the sub-tenants are suitable. They might be carrying out illegal activities such as a cannabis farm, or be operating as an unlicensed HMO, without the landlord's knowledge. They might also be letting it on Airbnb, leading to higher wear and tear and possibly in breach of the landlord's mortgage or insurance.

This is why regular inspections are so important, and most insurance policies require them.

How to authorise sub-letting

The default position

Tenancy agreements invariably contain a clause which says that the tenant cannot sub-let without the landlord's consent. If the agreement is silent, section 15 of the Housing Act 1988 states it is an implied term of periodic tenancies that a tenant cannot sub-let a property without the consent of the landlord.

This is because allowing a tenant to sub-let carries risk for the landlord, and may even be prohibited or restricted by a lender or insurance. If authorised sub-letting leads to the property becoming an unlicensed HMO, for example, the landlord will be liable for a rent repayment order.

The tenant's obligations as an intermediate landlord

With sub-letting, the tenant becomes the landlord of the sub-tenant and is responsible for carrying out the Right to Rent checks and other landlord obligations.

The tenant also remains liable to the landlord under the tenancy agreement to pay the rent and to look after the property in a tenant-like manner.

Checks before authorising a sub-let

Before authorising a tenant to sub-let, a landlord should insist on being able to carry out Right to Rent checks and the same referencing checks as they would for new tenants.

To avoid any disputes over the condition of the property, the landlord or agent should visit the property before the sub-tenant moves in to check the property and take photos. They should also insist on an inspection visit within four weeks of the start of the sub-tenancy to make sure all is in order.

The sub-letting addendum

In order to authorise a tenant to sub-let, the landlord should enter into an addendum to the tenancy agreement to approve the sub-letting, which contains an acknowledgement from the tenant that they are still liable under the tenancy agreement and will continue to pay the rent.

The addendum should also require the sub-tenancy agreement to contain the same obligations on the sub-tenant as are on the tenant in the original tenancy agreement.

How to spot unauthorised sub-letting

It's important for landlords or their agents to carry out regular inspections to check for unauthorised sub-letting (as well as checking the condition of the property). It's also a good idea to introduce yourself to the neighbours, as they can be well-placed to spot if unauthorised sub-letting is taking place.

Here is a list of things to look for on an inspection that may suggest the tenant may be sub-letting without permission from the landlord:

- Locks on bedroom doors and kitchen cabinets when the property is a single let to a single household (a couple or family).
- A key safe has been installed outside the property without good reason, e.g. for a dog walker or childcare, as it may be a sign that the property is being let on Airbnb.
- The tenant refuses access or inspections.
- The tenant is hard to contact and is always away.
- Higher than average wear and tear that is more than you'd expect with the tenants you let to.
- Signs of more people living / staying at the property than are in the tenancy agreement, e.g. extra bedding, lots of belongings in suitcases.
- Cooking equipment (microwave, kettle, fridge) in bedrooms when it's let to a single household and not as an HMO.
- The rent is paid by someone who is not listed in the tenancy agreement.
- Post addressed to people who are not and have never been tenants.

4. Pets

The RRA gives tenants an implied right to keep a pet, provided that they follow the statutory procedure to request a pet and the landlord doesn't have a good reason to turn down the request.

Process for a tenant to ask a landlord to keep a pet

This is the statutory process under section 16A Housing Act 1988, introduced by section 11 RRA, that a tenant will need to follow if they would like to keep a pet:

- The tenant must apply in writing to the landlord with a description of the pet for which consent is sought.
- The landlord must either give or refuse consent in writing within 28 days of the date of the request.
- The landlord may ask for further information if it's reasonable, and the deadline for responding will be seven days after the tenant provides the information to the landlord. If the tenant doesn't provide the information, the landlord doesn't need to give or refuse consent.
- If the landlord needs consent of a "superior landlord" (for instance, if they are a leaseholder and need the permission of the freeholder) and they apply for consent within 28 days of the tenant's request, they can delay giving or refusing consent until seven days following consent or refusal from the superior landlord.

Reasonable grounds for a landlord to refuse consent

There is no one-size-fits-all list of reasonable grounds, and landlords need to consider requests on their merits on a case-by-case basis.

The RRA specifically states that a landlord of leasehold property (e.g. a flat) may refuse a request if the lease prohibits it or if the freeholder or other superior landlord refuses to give consent, provided that they have taken "reasonable steps" to obtain that consent.

Here is a list of other reasons that might justify a landlord refusing consent, depending on the context:

- The type of pet is not appropriate for the property, e.g. a Great Dane in a studio flat.
- The number of pets is too high for the property, e.g. three dogs in a small flat.
- The landlord has reasonable concerns about the welfare of the pet, e.g. a request to keep a dog when the tenants do not work from home and/or the dog will be left for more than four hours a day on a regular basis.
- The landlord has good reason to believe the tenant will not be a responsible pet owner, e.g. after failing a home visit by an appropriate organisation.
- The landlord has an allergy to the pet in question and they self-manage.
- The tenant lives in an HMO, unless it is a joint tenancy and all tenants agree to keeping the pet.

Tenants' rights of appeal

If a tenant believes that their landlord has unreasonably refused their request for a pet, they can appeal against a refusal by escalating a complaint to the PRS Ombudsman (once launched) or by taking the case to court.

Both parties will be able to submit evidence to the Ombudsman or judge, who will then consider the evidence and decide what is right on the merits of the case.

Insurance against pet damage

It remains a prohibited payment under the Tenant Fees Act for a landlord to require a tenant to take out or pay for insurance against the risk of pet damage.

How to minimise the risk of pet damage

Being open to pets

I'm a pet-friendly landlord and am happy for tenants to have a dog or a cat in my properties, within reason, provided I believe that the tenants will be responsible pet owners and the pet or pets are suitable for the property.

The right in the RRA technically only applies to tenants rather than applicants, but if your property is potentially suitable, I believe it's better to be open at the start and say you'll consider applications from applicants with pets.

Referencing and meeting the pet

Insist on asking for a pet reference from both the current landlord and the previous landlord. Ideally, meet the pet to see how they behave, although this is easier with a dog than a cat.

The check-in inventory

Landlords should always get a check-in inventory anyway with clear photos of every part of the property, including the garden, but it is even more important when someone has a pet.

Without this, it may be difficult to prove what condition the property and garden were in when they moved in.

Pet Policy

Have a Pet Policy to make clear your expectations, and ask your tenant or prospective tenant to agree to it before you give permission to have a pet.

The tenancy agreement should say that the tenant accepts responsibility for the control, care and cleaning of the pet, and that they will repair any damage their pet causes.

Cleaning at the end of the tenancy

Landlords cannot insist that tenants use a professional cleaning service at the end of the tenancy, as that would infringe the Tenant Fees Act 2019 because it's a condition that they can only meet by paying a fee for a third-party service.

However, do make it a condition that they need to clean the property and carpets to a "professional standard", which is permitted if they property and carpets had been cleaned to a professional standard before the tenants moved in.

Now we have covered the common problems that arise in a tenancy, the next chapter is on how to carry out effective inspections, which reduce the risks of small issues becoming large problems.

CHAPTER 13

INSPECTIONS

Inspections are a vital part of managing rental properties. In this chapter, I explain the rationale behind carrying out regular inspections and explain the differences between inspections for single let properties and HMOs.

1. Why carry out regular inspections?

As mentioned above, section 9A of the Landlord and Tenant Act 1985 obliges landlords to make sure their property is in good condition and free of potentially harmful hazards, both at the start of the tenancy and throughout.

It's also likely to be a condition of your insurance policy that you carry out inspections as permitted under the tenancy agreement.

If a property falls into disrepair and the landlord doesn't attend to the repairs, the tenants will have the right to bring legal action against their landlord.

Catching problems early

It's in the interest of both tenants and landlords for a property to be kept in good repair, and regular inspections are a good way of keeping an eye on the condition of the property.

Tenants are often reluctant to report seemingly minor issues like a leaking tap, which may quickly become big issues if the tap is not repaired or replaced. Yet, it's vital to find out what needs repairing, as it's usually cheaper and easier to fix a small leak, than wait until it's a big leak that has caused joists to rot and mould to set in.

Inspections provide an opportunity for the landlord to check if there have been any breaches of the tenancy agreement, e.g. evidence of smoking inside, unauthorised sub-letting, unauthorised occupants or illegal activity. As discussed above, sub-letting can expose a landlord to lots of risks, including turning the property into an unlicensed HMO. It's therefore important to look out for the signs of sub-letting during the visit.

Setting expectations

Landlords should let prospective tenants know at the viewing stage how often they carry out inspection visits to keep on top of repairs. This sets expectations from the start and might discourage someone who is looking to sub-let without permission from going forward with the letting.

Also, when tenants see how the property should be maintained, there are fewer surprises at check-out when deductions from the deposit are considered. Encourage tenants to mention niggling issues, as it's far better to know about problems early.

It's also an opportunity for the landlord or agent to give practical advice, such as how to reduce condensation or how to prune the shrubs in the garden.

WHY I PREFER "MAINTENANCE VISITS"

I don't like the term "inspection", as it sounds adversarial.

I always arrange the first "maintenance visit" for a couple of weeks after they move in. I explain that I do this extra visit as often tenants spot little repair jobs that have been missed, and I like to make it easier for them to report them to me.

This helps us start the tenancy off on the right foot, and the tenants see that my focus is on keeping the property in good condition.

HMOs

Inspections are particularly important for HMOs, where HMO managers are subject to onerous obligations under the HMO Management Regulations, as discussed in Chapter 11.

Regular inspections help HMO managers demonstrate compliance and identify issues before the local authority does.

2. Single let inspections

The purpose of an inspection is to see whether the tenant is taking good care of the property and whether the property needs any maintenance. It's a key aspect of looking after your property and the people who live there.

In this section, I discuss tips on how to carry out successful inspections for single let properties.

How to arrange inspections for single lets

Section 11 of the Landlord and Tenant Act 1985 states that there is an implied covenant in every tenancy that the landlord or their authorised representative may enter the property at reasonable times of the day to view their "condition and state of repair" by giving 24 hours' written notice to the tenant.

In practice, 24 hours is not much notice, and it's likely to irritate tenants if a landlord or agent insists on 24 hours' notice, unless it is a genuine emergency.

Instead, I contact the tenants by WhatsApp at least a week in advance and offer different times that I think may work with their schedule for my maintenance visit. They let me know when is convenient for them, and if none of the times are suitable, I ask them to let me know when would be convenient.

They're already expecting that I'll be in contact, as I make it clear at the start of the tenancy that I do maintenance visits roughly every six months.

I think that giving them the option of different times and dates shows that I respect that they have their own commitments and that I'm happy to be flexible. I've never had a problem arranging inspections with this approach.

How often should inspections be?

After the initial visit a couple of weeks in, inspect single lets at least every six months to see the property in both winter and summer conditions. Damp and mould are harder to spot in summer; conversely, gardens can quickly become overgrown then.

If your agent's standard fee only covers one inspection, negotiate a second. The additional cost is usually minimal.

Do check your insurance policy, as some insurance policies exclude liability for loss or damage arising out of cannabis farms and other drug production if the landlord or agent does not inspect the property "every three months or as permitted under the tenancy agreement".

Even if a landlord outsources property management to an agent, it's a good idea for them to accompany the agent on one inspection a year so they can see for themselves how the letting agent and tenant are both looking after the property.

What if tenants won't give access?

Well-drafted tenancy agreements will have a clause that requires tenants to allow the landlord, agent or a contractor to have access to the property to inspect its condition or to carry out maintenance, repairs and improvements.

If the tenant refuses to allow entry, as well as being a breach of the implied covenant in the Landlord and Tenant Act 1985, it will be a breach of contract. This enables the landlord to claim damages from the tenant by charging them any reasonable costs incurred because of their refusal to agree to a request for access. For instance, if a gas engineer charges the landlord a call-out charge, if a tenant refuses access, it would be reasonable for the landlord to reclaim the wasted call-out charge from the tenant.

Claiming costs from tenants

As explained in the section on tenant fees in Chapter 9, claims for damages are permitted under the Tenant Fees Act 2019, so long as they are based on the actual loss that the landlord incurred because of the contractual breach.

However, landlords and agents cannot charge an automatic fee that isn't contingent on the landlord having suffered a loss. For instance, a term that says that the tenant must pay £50 for a missed appointment with a contractor is likely to be both an unfair term under the Consumer Rights Act 2015 and a breach of the Tenant Fees Act.

Although the landlord can claim damages for the breach of contract, they don't have the legal right to enter the premises without the tenant's permission, unless it's a genuine emergency, e.g. to let in a plumber to fix a burst water pipe or a gas engineer to repair a gas leak.

Keeping records

The landlord or agent should keep a record of the refusal in case the tenant later complains that the property is in disrepair, or as evidence for a claim for possession under Ground 12 (see Chapter 15 for more details of the grounds for possession under section 8 HA88).

What to do if a tenant refuses access

If the tenant refuses to grant access, the landlord or letting agent should try and find out why by texting or calling. There may be a perfectly good reason why the tenant has not responded.

However, if they don't get back in touch or allow access, the landlord or agent should send a formal letter to ask for access for an inspection. A more assertive follow-up letter could mention that landlords have the right to carry out inspections under section 11 of the Landlord and Tenant Act 1985 and that you will hold them personally liable for any additional costs if the condition of your property worsens during a period when you don't have access to carry out an inspection or repairs.

You could add that you may have no choice other than to take legal steps to recover possession of the property due to their breach of a material term in the tenancy agreement if they don't allow access.

If the tenant ignores these letters, apart from going to court to get an injunction which will order the tenant to allow access, the only other option is to seek possession of the property.

Repossession as a last resort

Repossession is harder now that section 21 has been abolished.

However, the landlord can use section 8, Ground 12, a discretionary ground which entitles a landlord to seek possession if a tenant breaches a term in the tenancy agreement.

There is also Ground 13, where the condition of the building and any common parts have "deteriorated owing to acts of waste by or the neglect or default of" the tenant, a member of the tenant's family or someone else living there.

As these are both discretionary grounds, the court has discretion whether to grant possession and will consider what is reasonable in the circumstances.

However, it's likely that the court will be sympathetic if you have acted reasonably and sent formal letters, particularly if they have also refused to allow a gas engineer to carry out the annual gas safety check.

The inspection

When you carry out an inspection, take a copy of your original inventory and the report from the last inspection with you, together with a note of any follow-up actions you have taken (e.g. repairs).

Be sure to take photos of anything that needs repair or maintenance as you carry out the inspection, even if it's the tenant's responsibility, and add the photos to your written record of the inspection. This may be useful in the event of an insurance claim or legal action. Letting agents will usually do this using software.

The key things to look out for when carrying out an inspection are the following:

Signs of damp and mould

Mould is often found in kitchens, bathrooms and bedrooms, so take a close look for the signs on the walls, or a musty smell. It's worth looking behind furniture that's up against outside walls. Ask the tenants as well if there is any mould or damp patches.

It's the landlord's responsibility to work out the underlying causes of damp and mould, such as structural issues or inadequate ventilation. For instance, has the ventilation been sealed up, causing damp? Are the trickle vents open in the UPVC windows in the cellar to help ventilation? Can you see signs of a roof leak or blocked drains? Do they dry clothes on radiators? Are they keeping the bathroom clean?

Likewise, maybe the tenant needs help in understanding the importance of ventilation and heating, and how to prevent mould in the shower or bath.

For more information on damp and mould, see Chapter 12.

Looking out for maintenance

Go around with a critical eye to see what either needs repair immediately, such as a leaking valley gutter, leaks and sealant that needs replacing, or what needs to go on your longer-term maintenance list, for instance repointing brickwork or replacing windows.

Do also point out repairs and maintenance that tenants need to do themselves, such as damage beyond reasonable wear and tear, and maintaining the garden properly, unless the tenancy agreement says the landlord will arrange this. I go through this in Chapter 3.

Poor cleanliness

The tenant is obliged to return the property at the end of the tenancy in the same state of cleanliness as it was at the beginning of the tenancy.

Dirty carpets will wear out more quickly, and stains tend to be harder to remove the longer they are left. Bathrooms and kitchens need to be kept clean, including wiping away any mould.

Don't forget to check the state of the cellar or loft, where rubbish can lead to vermin or even hide a cannabis farm!

Signs of pest infestation

Mice, rats, maggots and other pests can be a problem in rental properties, particularly if the tenant isn't disposing of their waste appropriately.

It's important to check for signs of a potential infestation and the source, e.g. food in the recycling bin, rubbish piling up in the garden, loft or cellar.

I go into dealing with pests and vermin in more detail in Chapter 12.

Signs of unauthorised sub-letting

Unauthorised sub-letting exposes a landlord to a lot of risk, including criminal behaviour, an unlicensed HMO, extra wear and tear if the tenant is running an Airbnb-style operation, and even a rent-to-rent scam in which the tenant pockets a premium from sub-tenants while falling behind on your rent.

You can read about the signs of unauthorised sub-letting in Chapter 12.

Inspection reports

Keep a detailed report of each inspection, with photographs of any problems you spot during an inspection, together with a note of any conversation with the tenant about the problems, and how they will be resolved. Not only may it be a requirement of your insurance to keep a written record of inspections, but it will be a contemporaneous note that may be useful in the event of prosecution or a dispute.

Here is a summary of what to include in an inspection report:

- Summary of next steps from previous inspection, and whether they have been addressed. If not, detail further steps.
- Are there any breaches of the tenancy agreement? Yes / No. Your observations. Comments by tenant. Next steps.
- Any damage caused by the tenants? Yes (beyond reasonable wear and tear) / Yes (reasonable wear and tear) / No. Your observations (including photos). Comments by tenant. What you said to the tenants. Next steps.
- Are the tenants taking proper care of the property? Yes / No. If no, your observations (including photos). Comments by tenants. Instructions given by you to tenants. Next steps.
- List of repairs required.
- Anything raised by tenant.
- Summary of advice given to tenants, e.g. how to reduce condensation, tips to maintain garden.
- Summary of next steps from this visit, e.g. follow-up inspection, arrange repairs.

Following up

Always write to your tenants to confirm whether the inspection revealed any issues which need addressing (e.g. repairs, damage, breach of contract), and to record any instructions you gave them. If everything was in order, or if just a minor repair is needed, you can send an informal WhatsApp message.

For instance, you can confirm that everything was in order other than the dripping tap in the kitchen, which you'll get repaired. If there are more serious issues, send a formal letter which details any areas of concern and spells out what they need to do or what action you will take.

Be sure to follow up on the next steps outlined in your inspection report; for instance, book in the repairs or arrange a follow-up inspection. You should review this before your next inspection and summarise in the next report whether the actions have been addressed.

3. HMO inspections

It is tempting to think that the rules of HMOs are the same as they are for single household buy-to-lets. However, this isn't the case, as HMOs are subject to higher standards than single lets, due to the HMO Management Regulations, which I explained in Chapter 11.

In this section, I explain the nuts and bolts of carrying out inspections for HMOs.

How often should inspections be for HMOs?

Assessing the right frequency

An experienced property manager will be able to advise on the appropriate frequency of inspections for HMOs.

If you're managing an HMO yourself, start by carrying out a short risk assessment on the property. This can be revised if, say, the tenants are exceptionally clean and tidy, or the opposite. The larger the HMO or the more vulnerable the tenants, the greater the likelihood that the inspections will need to be more frequent.

The frequency of inspections also depends on whether the landlord provides a cleaner. Six-monthly formal inspections may be appropriate for a small HMO where the tenants look after the property well and a cleaner cleans the common parts once a fortnight and keeps an eye on repairs. On the other hand, weekly visits might be appropriate for tenants with social, educational or mental health issues.

Providing cleaners and gardeners for HMOs

The reason why HMO landlords often provide cleaners is because the HMO Management Regulations require landlords/managers to keep things in "clean" order. This is particularly common where tenants rent on an individual room basis.

It's less common to provide cleaners where a group of people rent a property together on a single tenancy agreement as joint tenants, such as students. This is because they're more likely to know each other and agree the cleaning among themselves.

As well as cleaning the common parts, cleaners can keep an eye on those common parts, in between the more formal inspections. For instance, they check that the hallways and stairs are free of obstacles, whether anything needs repair, put out the bins, and test the fire alarm according to the requirements of the HMO licence.

Some HMO landlords provide a gardener to take care of the garden.

The cleaner or gardener should write a short note each time they visit and highlight any issues, e.g. a bike in a hallway, disrepair, fire doors that are jammed open, covered up vents and smoke alarms, broken taps, broken handles, etc, so that the manager can follow up with the tenants.

Some HMO landlords ask their cleaners to take videos of the common parts each visit to record the condition of the property. This might seem like overkill, but it depends on the risk.

Keeping a log

The manager should keep a log of any action taken, including the reports from any cleaner or gardener.

Having an effective system will enable you to show the local authority that you manage the HMO proactively if they ever bring a prosecution for breach of the HMO Management Regulations or the terms of the licence.

What if HMO tenants won't give access?

The landlord or contractor of an HMO let on an individual room basis has the right to enter the common parts to carry out repairing and cleaning obligations (but needs the permission of the relevant tenant to enter an individual bedroom).

Where the cleaner has a regular schedule, they should tell the tenants which days the cleaner will come (e.g. every other Wednesday morning).

For maintenance and inspections of the common parts, they should give 24 hours' notice and come at reasonable times, unless it's an emergency. This means that tenants who rent on a room basis cannot stop a landlord or contractor from having access to the common parts, although the landlord should be respectful and give notice.

In terms of access to the individual bedrooms and bedsits, or the whole HMO if the tenants rent under a joint tenancy, the law is the same as for single lets (see above). Landlords must give at least 24 hours' notice and cannot let themselves in without the permission of the tenants.

Following up

As HMO landlords and managers can be prosecuted under the HMO Management Regulations, it's particularly important for them to keep clear evidence of regular inspections and visits, including visits by cleaners and maintenance staff.

Having a written record of inspections and other visits with photographs and follow-up actions will be valuable evidence of your compliance with the regulations in the event of enforcement action by the local council. For instance, if a cleaner notices a bike blocking the hallway, keep a record of the photo of the bike, a copy of the message to the tenants and a follow-up check a week later to make sure the bike has been moved.

The final chapter of Part III is on the rules relating to rent once the tenancy has started.

CHAPTER 14

RENT

The RRA introduced significant changes to the rules relating to rent for assured periodic tenancies.

We looked at the rules relating to rent for the period before a tenancy starts in Chapter 6. The focus of this chapter is on the rules about rent during a tenancy, including the payment of rent in advance, increasing rent and how landlords can manage rent arrears proactively.

1. Rent payable in advance during a tenancy

Any clause in a new assured periodic tenancy agreement after 1 May 2026 that requires a tenant to pay rent before the start of a rent period to which it relates is unenforceable. For instance, a clause requiring the tenant to pay six months' rent on the first day of the tenancy would be void, as rent periods cannot be more than one month, and landlords cannot require tenants to pay rent for multiple rent periods at a time.

This is because the new section 4B Housing Act 1988 states that any terms in tenancy agreements that provide for the payment of rent in advance, other than the initial rent discussed above, have "no effect".

A landlord may accept rent in advance during a tenancy if the tenant voluntarily wishes to pay it before it is due; for instance, a student who wishes to pay by the term or the quarter. However, as explained in Chapter 6, it will be a prohibited pre-tenancy rent payment if the landlord or agent asks the tenant to pay rent or if they accept an unsolicited payment of rent before the tenancy agreement is entered into.

A new section 14ZC of the Housing Act 1988 states that a landlord must repay any rent paid in advance that relates to days falling after the end of a tenancy; for example, if the tenant pays a year in advance, but leaves after six months.

2. Increasing rent during a tenancy

Section 13 procedure

The RRA makes it compulsory for landlords to use the procedure under section 13 of the Housing Act 1988 if they wish to increase rent for tenants. There is no other way to do it for assured periodic tenancies.

Note that this only applies to APTs. If your tenancy falls outside the Housing Act 1988, for example a high-rent tenancy or a company let, section 13 doesn't apply and you can increase the rent in accordance with whatever mechanism is in the tenancy agreement.

This means that rent review clauses in old assured shorthold tenancy agreements, and new assured periodic tenancy agreements, are null and void.

It is also no longer possible to agree a rent increase informally. As all tenancies are periodic, the annual "renewal" cycle ended. Agents often used the renewal of fixed-term tenancies to increase the rent.

The only way to increase rent for an APT now is by serving a section 13 notice, using the new Form 4A, which is available on the Government website.[1]

Landlords must serve Form 4A at least two months before they propose the new rent to come into force. The date of the new rent should coincide with "the beginning of a new period of the tenancy".

Once the section 13 notice is served, it's possible for the landlord or letting agent to negotiate a lower rent than the amount in the notice and agree that in writing via an amendment or addendum.

Tenants' rights to challenge a section 13 rent increase

If the tenant is unhappy with the rent increase proposed in the section 13 notice, they have the option of referring the rent to the First-tier Tribunal (FTT) before the date the rent increase is due to start for the tribunal to determine what the market rent for the property is.

The rent increase will be delayed until the FTT has made its determination. The FTT only has the power to keep the rent increase to the level in the notice or to reduce it to the higher of the open market rent and the existing tenancy rent. It cannot set a rent that is higher than the amount in the notice, even if they determine the open-market rent is higher.

The landlord must wait another 12 months from the date that

1. Ministry of Housing, Communities and Local Government, *Assured Tenancy Forms*, https://www.gov.uk/guidance/assured-tenancy-forms.

the new rent comes into force before they can increase the rent using section 13 again.

The tenant must pay a small fee to challenge a rent increase at the FTT. If the landlord wins, however, they won't be able to claim costs from the tenant.

3. Avoiding and managing rent arrears

Sometimes tenants fall behind with their rent. If they don't pay the full rent when due, they are said to be "in rent arrears".

Managing rent arrears is a difficult aspect of being a landlord, even if it's outsourced to a letting agent.

Prevention is very much better than cure, and early empathetic intervention from the landlord or agent can help the tenant and prevent arrears from escalating. It's important to keep on top of rent payments, and manage any rent arrears actively, to try to avoid eviction for non-payment of rent.

Choose the right rent due date

There is no standard date on which everyone is paid in England, and for those who are paid on a calendar month basis, it tends to range from the 20th of the month to the last day of the month, or even the last Friday. The 25th is a very common date in my experience.

The first action at the start of the tenancy is therefore to discuss the best date for the tenants to pay their rent, and this will usually be the day after they receive their wages from their employer, when they are more likely to have money in their account. If this date is the 25th of each month, yet rent is due on the 20th, they're more likely to fall into rent arrears than if rent is due on the 27th.

For joint tenants, the best date might be just after both or all have been paid. If your tenants receive benefits, be aware that they are paid on a four-weekly or fortnightly basis and won't ever be in sync with calendar months.

Some letting agents and landlords like to have all rent paid on the same day for ease of administration. This is often the 1st of the month.

Changing the rent payment date

If the chosen rent payment date doesn't align with the first day of the rent period, you'll need to change the rent payment date. However, the Renters' Rights Act has made this more complicated.

If you change the rent payment date at the start of the tenancy, be aware that the initial rent payment cannot be for more than the rent for one calendar month. This means that the first rent payment might be a small balancing amount, before you move to the regular rent payment date to suit the tenants.

Tenants may ask to change the rent payment date if they move jobs, which is something that a landlord should agree to, assuming they can prove this. It's easy to record this change by an addendum to the tenancy agreement, or even a letter signed by both parties.

It is possible to charge tenants £50 to change the payment date under the Tenant Fees Act 2019, but this is not something I do as a self-managing landlord.

Ask tenants to set up standing order

When you check in your tenants (if self-managing), ask them to set up a standing order for the rent and to let you know when they have done this. I message them my bank details as well as including the payment information in my welcome pack. By having a standing order in place, you're not reliant on the tenant remembering to pay the rent.

When I do the maintenance visit a couple of weeks into the new tenancy, I ask if they've set up the standing order, and provide them with my bank details again if they haven't. If the payment doesn't arrive in your bank account first thing on the allotted day, they haven't set up a standing order.

The tenant will need to change the standing order when the rent increases.

Track rent payments every month

An important part of running a business is to keep a close eye on cash flow. This is just as true for landlords as it is for other businesses.

I check my bank account on the date the rent is due from my tenants (currently the 25th). If the date falls on the weekend or a Bank Holiday, I treat the rent as being due on the first working day after that.

If you use an agent, make clear you want them to advise you if the rent is not paid within (say) five working days of the due date. Another way to track rent is to use online accountancy software or property management software which is linked to your bank account.

Helping your tenant if they fall into arrears

Tenants fall behind with their rent for many reasons, and the first reaction of a good landlord should be to speak to the tenant to find out why and how long their financial difficulties are likely to last. It might be a temporary blip, in which case a payment plan might be appropriate.

Conversely, the cause may be serious – for example, if they've lost their job, had their hours cut or been unable to work due to health issues.

They may also not realise that they're entitled to benefits such as Universal Credit. The Entitled To website[2] has an excellent online benefits calculator which will show if your tenant is eligible for other support.

However, it can take at least five weeks for the tenant to receive their first payment after they submit a claim for Universal Credit. It's also possible for landlords to apply to have Universal Credit paid directly to them if their tenant has at least two months' rent arrears.

If your tenant needs advice on debt, suggest they contact the Citizens Advice debt helpline: (0800 144 8848). Another excellent source of help is Shelter.

Breathing Space

Breathing Space is a government scheme that provides people in debt with time to receive debt advice and try to find a way forward.

2. See https://www.entitledto.co.uk/.

If a debt advisor tells you that your tenant has entered into a breathing space, you're not allowed to take action to collect or enforce their rent arrears until the breathing space period ends. The standard breathing space period is 60 days and a mental health crisis breathing space lasts as long as their treatment for their crisis, plus 30 days.

For further details, see the *Debt Respite Scheme (Breathing Space) Guidance for Creditors* published by the Insolvency Service.[3] There is more information on Breathing Space in Chapter 15.

Charging interest on late payments

Landlords can charge interest if the tenancy agreement entitles them to do so, and the amount cannot be more than 3% above base rate. However, the rent must have been outstanding for 14 days. Once the 14 days have passed, they can backdate it to the day the rent fell due until it is paid in full.

When the 14 days have passed since the rent was due, it is appropriate to send a second formal reminder letter which advises them they are now accruing a late-payment fee on their debt.

There are online calculators for the default late-payment fee,[4] but you can calculate the daily late-payment fee and the total late-payment fee yourself using this formula:

3. The Insolvency Service, *Debt Respite Scheme (Breathing Space) Guidance for Creditors*,https://www.gov.uk/government/publications/debt-respite-scheme-breathing-space-guidance/debt-respite-scheme-breathing-space-guidance-for-creditors.

4. For instance, this *Interest Calculator* by New Square Chambers: https://newsquarechambers.co.uk/calculators-publications/interest-calculator.

THE DAILY LATE-PAYMENT FEE CALCULATION

Interest rate (A%) = base rate + 3%

Daily late-payment fee (£B) = (amount of arrears x A%) / 365

Total late-payment fee (£C) = number of days in arrears × £B

Total rent arrears (£D) = £C + amount of arrears

Clearly, it's more complicated to calculate if more than one month's rent is due, but this shows you the principles.

Late-payment process

If a tenant falls behind with their rent payments, the landlord or agent should follow a process to try to help the tenant make up the shortfall before it gets out of hand.

Although there is no obligation on a landlord to issue reminders or chase payments, it's good practice to do so.

It's important to keep records of any conversations you have with the tenant about their arrears or a payment plan, and to confirm what was discussed and agreed by a follow-up email. Also, if the tenant falls into arrears, make sure you advise the guarantor, and send them copies of the letters you send the tenant.

Overview of process

Here is an overview of a simple late-payment process that escalates from a friendly reminder via text to the step before issuing a letter before claim:

EXAMPLE OF LATE PAYMENT PROCESS

1 day overdue. Friendly text – Note missed payment, ask if everything is OK, suggest standing order

2-4 days overdue. Follow-up text – Slightly more formal, ask them to pay or call to discuss, mention support available

7 days overdue. First letter – State arrears amount, note interest will accrue from day 14, request payment by [date]

15 days overdue. Second letter - Confirm interest now accruing, give calculation, request payment within seven days. State that the next step is a letter before claim

Letter before claim

A landlord must send a letter before claim before commencing legal action. Send it one week after the second letter.

The letter before claim is a final warning before you start debt collection in the County Court to obtain a County Court Judgment (CCJ) being listed against their name and/or before you commence possession proceedings under section 8.

The letter before action should include the full details of the debt, the interest, the method of payment and a reply form. You can also add that legal action may result in a CCJ in their name, which will impact their credit rating and make it difficult for them to obtain credit or finance for at least six years, and that continued non-payment may lead to eviction.

Do stress in the letter that you will consider a reasonable payment plan and/or mediation and provide them with the details of the Citizens Advice debt helpline: (0800 144 8848).

Applying for a CCJ in the County Court

If you succeed in obtaining an order for possession under section 8, you will get a money judgment for the rent arrears due as of the date of the hearing, provided you include this in your claim. It's not automatic.

You may also apply for a County Court Judgment (CCJ) if your tenant is still living in the property or if they move out without you obtaining an order for possession.

Here's a link to the Government website advice on bringing a claim in the County Court.[5]

This brings us to the end of Part III, and we now move on to Part IV, which deals with the end of the tenancy.

5. GOV.UK, *Make a Court Claim for Money*, https://www.gov.uk/make-court-claim-for-money.

PART IV

ENDING THE TENANCY

CHAPTER 15

TERMINATING A TENANCY

In this chapter, I explain how a tenant and a landlord can each end a tenancy, and give tips to help with the practicalities of ensuring a smooth check-out process when the tenant moves out.

1. Termination by tenant

Tenant notice to quit

The end of fixed terms

As explained in Chapter 2, the RRA abolished fixed terms for assured shorthold tenancies, and all existing ASTs with a fixed term became assured periodic tenancies on 1 May 2026, with no fixed term or end date.

Assured periodic tenancies are, by their very nature, periodic and without a fixed term, and it is a breach of section 16E Housing Act 1988 to "purport to let for a fixed term".

This means that a tenant is no longer locked into an APT for a set period.

Instead, they can end a tenancy at any time once the tenancy has started by serving a notice to quit to the landlord (or the letting agent) that gives at least two months' notice, with the notice to expire at the end of a rent period or the day after, in accordance with established case law.[1]

The notice period will be less if the landlord agrees, for instance in the tenancy agreement.

How notice to quit can be given

The landlord cannot insist that the tenant send the notice in a particular format or method of delivery.

In fact, the government guidance says that a tenant can give a notice to quit by email, letter and even text.[2]

Joint tenants

If the tenancy is a joint tenancy (two or more tenants on the tenancy) and one tenant serves a notice to quit, it will bring the tenancy to an end for all of the tenants.

The notice to quit can only be withdrawn if all the tenants and the landlord agree.

Waiving the notice period

The landlord can agree to waive some or all the notice period, should they wish.

---

1. For instance, see the Court of Appeal case of *Sidebotham v Holland* [1895] 1 QB 378, https://babel.hathitrust.org/cgi/pt?id=umn.31951002535901h&seq=427.
2. Ministry of Housing, Communities and Local Government, *Renting out Your Property: Guidance for Landlords and Letting Agents – If Your Tenant Wants to Leave*, https://www.gov.uk/guidance/renting-out-your-property-guidance-for-landlords-and-letting-agents/if-your-tenant-wants-to-leave.

However, where there are joint tenants, all the tenants need to agree that the notice given is to be less than two months.

What if the tenant abandons the property?

Unless the tenant surrenders the tenancy, for instance by handing back the keys, landlords can't simply change the locks if it appears the tenants have moved out and have abandoned the property. They might just be on an extended holiday or away on business.

Instead, the landlord will need to use the section 8 procedure to obtain possession, which is likely to be uncontested by the tenant if they have no intention of moving back. Usually this will be for rent arrears.

The notice should be served at the tenant's "usual or last-known residence", and until the tenancy is formally ended, that remains the rental property itself.

2. The end of section 21

The RRA abolished section 21 of the Housing Act 1988, which means that landlords can no longer give two months' notice to end a tenancy without needing to give a reason, often referred to as a "no fault eviction" notice.

What's more, the RRA introduced a new section 16E to the Housing Act 1988 which prohibits landlords and letting agents purporting to end a tenancy by serving a notice to quit, for instance by serving an old section 21 notice on the tenants, asking them to leave. They are also prevented from doing it orally.

The local housing authority can impose a civil penalty of up to £7,000 for a first-time breach.

It will be an offence if the breach continues or is repeated within five years, which means the local authority can impose a civil penalty of up to £40,000 and the tenants will be able apply for a rent repayment order at the First-tier Tribunal of up to two years' rent.

Consequently, it's very important not to attempt to serve a section 21 notice on tenants, even if the tenancy agreement says the landlord can serve a two month notice to quit. Not only is it illegal, but it may also result in you receiving a large civil penalty.

3. Termination by landlords under section 8

Landlords can only terminate an assured periodic tenancy by establishing one of the grounds for possession under section 8 of the Housing Act 1988 and serving the tenant with a valid Form 3A, available on the Assured Tenancy Forms section of the government website.[3]

Due to the complexity of possession proceedings, it is highly advisable to speak to a qualified specialist solicitor before trying to recover possession using section 8.

Serving a section 8 notice

Form 3A formally notifies the tenant that the landlord intends to seek possession and states the specific ground or grounds relied on, with a full explanation.

---

3. The *Assured Tenancy Forms* are available at: https://www.gov.uk/guidance/assured-tenancy-forms.

The form also needs to specify the earliest date on which possession proceedings can begin, and this notice period varies according to the grounds. It's usually two weeks, two months or four months after service of the notice. The notice period does not need to expire at the end of a rent period.

If there are multiple grounds, the longest notice period will generally apply. The section 8 notice won't be valid if the landlord doesn't give the correct amount of notice.

If the tenant doesn't leave

If the tenants don't move out voluntarily after the notice is served, the landlord will need to apply to court for an order for possession and provide evidence to the judge that they meet the criteria for the ground.

If you don't begin possession proceedings within 12 months of serving the notice, it will lapse, and you will need to start again.

Misuse of grounds

Landlords must not use a possession ground they don't qualify for. This is because it's an offence under section 16J of the Housing Act 1988 to use a possession ground knowing that they won't be able to get a court order for possession using that ground, or being "reckless" about it, if the tenant then surrenders the tenancy within four months, without a court order.

The former tenants will also be able to apply to the First-tier Tribunal for a rent repayment order that may require the landlord to repay up to two years' rent.

4. Mandatory grounds for possession

The mandatory grounds for possession are set out in Part 1 of Schedule 2 of the Housing Act 1988 and were amended by the RRA.

The word "mandatory" means that the court must order possession if the landlord can prove that the ground applies. Unlike the now defunct section 21, the landlord will need to provide evidence to show the court that they qualify for a ground. Once the court is satisfied that the landlord meets the ground, they have no choice but issue an order for possession.

Many of these mandatory grounds are also "no fault", in that they involve no fault on the part of the tenant, but are due to the plans of the landlord.

Here is a summary of the key mandatory grounds for possession for private landlords. Note that this is not a comprehensive summary. For instance, it doesn't include the many grounds relating to employment, supported housing and a council's homeless duty.

Ground 1 – Landlord or family moving in (four months' notice)

A landlord may recover possession if they, their spouse or civil partner and certain close family members wish to move into the property and use it as their "sole or principal home".

Who does and doesn't qualify?

The definition of family includes the landlord or their spouse or civil partner's children or grandchildren. It also covers the landlord's parent, grandparent or sibling, child or grandchild. This includes the curiously termed "half-blood" relations but does not include cousins or aunts and uncles.

However, if the landlord is a limited company, this ground will not be available to the shareholders, directors and their close family. This is because a company is a separate legal entity that is distinct from its shareholders and directors.

Timing

The landlord must provide at least four months' notice to the tenant if they wish to rely on Ground 1. They can serve the notice at any point, but the notice must not expire until the first year of the tenancy has passed.

For instance, if a landlord serves the notice after the 8th month of the tenancy, they can give four months' notice, as this will expire after the first year. If they serve it earlier, they will need to give more than four months' notice to ensure it expires after the first year.

Re-let ban during restricted period

After using Ground 1 (or Ground 1A), there is a restricted period during which a landlord cannot re-let the property or allow someone to live or stay there under a "licence to occupy" for money (e.g. using an online holiday let platform) or even market the property for letting or a licence to occupy.

Marketing includes a letting agent telling someone that the property is or may be available for let.

The restricted period begins when the section 8 notice is served and ends 12 months from the later of the date specified in the notice and the earliest date on which proceedings for possession will begin.

In practice, this means at least 16 months from the date the section 8 notice is served.

There is an exception where the landlord successfully obtains an order for possession during the restricted period for another ground, e.g. rent arrears. In that case, the restricted period will end on the date that order for possession is made.

Sanctions

The new section 16J HA88 makes it an offence for a landlord to let or market the property during the restricted period. It is also an offence for another to do it on their behalf, e.g. a letting agent, unless they can prove they took "all reasonable steps to avoid contravening it".

The local housing authority has the power to impose a civil penalty of up to £40,000 for an offence, and the tenants can apply to the First-tier Tribunal for a rent repayment order of up to two years' rent.

Ground 1A – Landlord selling up (four months' notice)

Ground 1A is available if a landlord can prove they "intend to sell the property".

As with Ground 1, the landlord will not be able to re-let the property, allow someone to live or stay there under a "licence to occupy" for money (e.g. Airbnb), or market the property for letting or a licence to occupy, for the same restricted period of 12 months, plus the notice period, which is a minimum of four months. It's also an offence to do so, subject to the same penalties as Ground 1.

Consequently, if a landlord is unable to sell the property after serving a section 8 notice relying on ground 1A, they will need to be prepared to receive no income from the property for at least 16 months.

There is an exception if a licence to occupy is granted to someone who is buying the property, and the licence is granted in anticipation of that purchase. There is another exception for shared-ownership leases.[4]

Before you decide to serve a notice to obtain vacant possession, it's worth speaking to the tenants to see if they wish to buy the property from you.

There are lots of resources to help tenants who wish to buy a property on the Tenant 2 Owner website.[5]

Ground 4A – Full-time students in HMO (four months' notice)

This is a very narrow ground that only applies to HMOs where all the tenants meet the "student test". To qualify for the student test, they must all be full-time students at the start of the tenancy on a higher education course, or the landlord has reasonable grounds to believe they will become full-time students during the tenancy.

The reference to HMOs includes all HMOs, whether or not they are licensed; in other words, where there are three or more occupiers from two or more households.

4. See section 16F (3) to (5) Housing Act 1988.
5. Tenant 2 Owner, https://www.tenant2owner.co.uk.

In order to be able to use Ground 4A, the following conditions must be fulfilled:

1. The landlord must have provided the tenants with a written statement of their wish to be able to recover possession on the basis that the tenants all met the student test at the start of the tenancy and that the landlord intends on the next occasion to let it to students who meet the student test.
2. The landlord must give at least four months' notice using Form 3A, with the notice to expire between 1 June and 30 September.
3. The landlord can't rely on this ground unless the tenancy was entered into no more than six months before the tenants were entitled to move in.
4. The landlord must intend to let the property to full-time students or those who the landlord believes will become full-time students during the tenancy.

If the tenants stop being full-time students during the tenancy, that will not remove the landlord's right to use Ground 4A. This is because the requirement is for the landlord to have had reasonable grounds at the start of the tenancy to believe that they would be full-time students during the tenancy.

Consequently, if one of the tenants drops out of university, but continues living in the house, or if they switch to a part-time course, the landlord will still be able to use Ground 4A.

Ground 6 – Redevelopment by landlord (four months' notice)

The landlord must show they "intend to demolish or reconstruct the whole or a substantial part of the dwelling-house or to carry out substantial works" to the whole or a considerable part of the property. Further, they must be able to show that the work can't be reasonably done while the tenants are living in the property.

An example might be a back-to-brick refurbishment to bring the property to an EPC C, or other substantial work.

Ground 6B – Enforcement action against landlord (four months' notice)

Ground 6B requires the court to award possession if the landlord needs to end a tenancy because it would be unlawful for them to maintain the tenancy due to enforcement action against them. For instance, a banning order, overcrowding, refusal or revocation of an HMO licence, or where the number of tenants exceeds the number in the HMO licence.

The court may order the landlord to pay compensation to the tenant "as appears sufficient as compensation for damage or loss sustained by that tenant as a result of the order for possession". The court must consider the circumstances which led to the enforcement action, "including any conduct by the tenant which caused or contributed to Ground 6B being available".

This could include if the tenant sub-let the property without the consent or knowledge of the landlord, causing it to be an unlicensed HMO, or overcrowding in breach of the terms of a licence.

Ground 7A – Serious anti-social behaviour (immediate)

Ground 7A enables a landlord to recover possession if at least one of five anti-social behaviour conditions are met, which I summarise below:

- **Conviction of a serious offence.** Conviction of a tenant, occupier or visitor to the property of a serious offence committed in the locality against someone who lives (or has the right to live) in the locality, the landlord or someone involved in the management of the landlord's properties.
- **Breach of an injunction.** A court must have found that a tenant, occupier or visitor to the property had breached an injunction to prevent nuisance or annoyance in the locality.
- **Breach of a criminal behaviour order.** Conviction of a criminal behaviour order that prohibits an activity in the locality by a tenant, occupier or visitor to the property. The order must have been intended to protect someone who lives in the locality (or has the right to), the landlord or someone involved in the management of the landlord's properties.
- **Closure order.** The property is, or has previously been, the subject of a closure order and entry to the property has been barred for a continuous period of at least 48 hours.
- **Noise nuisance.** The tenant, occupier or visitor has been convicted of breaching either an abatement

notice or a court order under the Environmental Protection Act 1990, and the offence related to excessive noise coming from the property amounted to a statutory nuisance.

The landlord cannot use any of the conditions for so long as there is a pending appeal against the relevant conviction, finding or order. Each condition has specific requirements, and I advise you to speak to a specialist solicitor if you are thinking of using this ground.

Ground 7B – No right to rent (two weeks' notice)

Ground 7B applies where the Home Office has served notice on the landlord that one or more of the tenants or occupiers in the property have no right to rent because of their immigration status.

Where there's a joint tenancy and the other tenant has a right to rent, the court may transfer the tenancy to that person.

Ground 8 – Serious rent arrears (four weeks' notice)

A landlord may rely on Ground 8 if there are rent arrears of at least three months' (or 13 weeks') rent at the date the landlord serves the notice and at the date of the hearing.

However, when calculating the amount of rent arrears for Ground 8, the landlord must ignore any amount that is unpaid solely because the tenant has not yet received their Universal Credit housing payment, assuming they are entitled to receive it.

5. Discretionary grounds for possession

Discretionary grounds are set out in Part 2 of Schedule 2 of the Housing Act 1988 and were also amended by the RRA.

With discretionary grounds, the judge will only grant the landlord possession if they are satisfied that the landlord has provided sufficient evidence to prove the ground applies and they believe that it is reasonable to grant the landlord possession in the circumstances.

The judge also has wide powers to postpone cases involving discretionary grounds.

Most of the discretionary grounds involve fault on the part of the tenant, for which the landlord will need to provide evidence.

Here is a summary of the key discretionary grounds for possession for private landlords. Again, it's not a comprehensive list of the grounds, and it's important to get specialist legal advice before relying on a ground.

Ground 10 – Any rent arrears (four weeks' notice)

This enables a landlord to seek possession if any rent is in arrears both at the time of the service of the notice and at the time of the court hearing.

This may be useful if the tenants keep the rent arrears just below the three months needed for Ground 8 for serious rent arrears.

Ground 11 – Persistent rent arrears (four weeks' notice)

This ground covers the situation where the tenant is persistently late in paying rent and, unlike Grounds 8 and 10, it applies even if no rent is outstanding at the date of the hearing.

Ground 12 – Breach of tenancy agreement (two weeks' notice)

Ground 12 applies where the tenant breaches a term in the tenancy agreement, other than rent.

It might include running a cannabis farm in the property, sub-letting without consent, or refusing to allow the landlord and their contractors access to the property to carry out an inspection or repairs in breach of the implied covenant in section 11 Landlord and Tenant Act 1985 or a clause in the tenancy agreement.

Ground 13 – Deterioration of the property (two weeks' notice)

A landlord can use Ground 13 where the condition of the building and any common parts have "deteriorated owing to acts of waste by or the neglect or default of" the tenant, a member of the tenant's family or someone else living there.

Ground 14 – Anti-social behaviour (immediate)

This ground covers a wider range of anti-social behaviour than Ground 7A, where a tenant, occupier or visitor to the property:

- Creates or is likely to create a nuisance or annoyance to neighbours, housemates (for instance in an HMO), anyone in the locality, the landlord or those managing the property.
- Has been convicted of using or permitting the use of the property for immoral or illegal purposes.
- Has been convicted of an indictable offence in the property or in the locality.

According to section 9A of the Housing Act 1988, the court must consider the following factors when deciding whether it is reasonable to grant an order for possession, including:

- The effect that the nuisance or annoyance has had on others
- The effect it's likely to have on others if it happens again
- Whether they have co-operated with any attempt by the landlord to encourage the conduct to stop.

Where a tenant in an HMO has committed any of the above, the court must "have particular regard to" the effect the behaviour has on those living in the HMO who share facilities with the tenant.

Ground 14ZA – Offence during a riot (two weeks' notice)

The court can order possession on ground 14ZA if it is satisfied that a tenant or an adult living in the property has been convicted in the Crown Court of a serious offence during a riot in the UK, as defined in section 1 of the Public Order Act 1986.

Ground 15 – Damage to furniture (two weeks' notice)

Ground 15 is similar to Ground 13, but it applies where the furniture provided by the landlord has been damaged through mistreatment by a tenant, occupier, lodger or sub-tenant.

In the case where it is a sub-tenant or a lodger who has caused the damage, the landlord will need to show the tenant did not take "reasonable steps expected to have that lodger or sub-tenant removed".

Ground 17 – False statement made by tenant (two weeks' notice)

This ground may be used if the landlord was "induced to grant the tenancy by a false statement made knowingly or recklessly by the tenant or someone acting at the tenant's instigation".

This includes the situation if the landlord has evidence that the tenant falsified a reference or lied about their circumstances.

6. How to serve a section 8 notice

The landlord must serve a separate section 8 notice (i.e. Form 3A) on each of the tenants and keep a copy.

It's important to keep evidence of serving the notice for use in court, if need be. It can be done in the manner specified in the tenancy agreement, which can be by hand, courier, registered post, regular first class post and even email.

If served by first class post, do try to minimise the likelihood of dispute as to whether or when it was sent. A simple way is to ask for a certificate of posting from the Post Office. Also, take a photo of you (or someone else) handing over the envelope at the Post Office. The law deems the notice to be served the second day after it was posted. If that's not a business day, it will be the next business day.

To serve the notice in person, it's best to go with a witness, and take a photo of the envelope being posted through the letter box of the property. If the tenant isn't at the property or refuses to acknowledge receipt, complete form N215, which is a certificate of service.[6]

If the tenant doesn't leave by the date specified in the notice, the landlord cannot go and evict the tenant themselves. Instead, they will need to obtain an order for possession from the court.

7. Recovering possession

After the landlord has served the section 8 notice, they must wait until the date stated in the notice has passed before going to court for an order for possession and enforcing the order for possession if the tenant does not move out voluntarily.

This section is a high-level overview of the steps and is not comprehensive. As this is a legal process, it is highly advisable to use a specialist solicitor to do this for you.

Breathing Space

Landlords must also not issue proceedings using the rent

6. HM Courts & Tribunal Service, *Certificate of Service in Civil Cases: Form N215*, https://www.gov.uk/government/publications/form-n215-certificate-of-service,

arrears grounds (Grounds 8, 10 or 11) if they've been notified the tenant is in a Breathing Space.

A standard breathing space is available to anyone with "problem debt" and it prevents landlords from issuing proceedings for up to 60 days. A mental health crisis breathing space will last for so long as the tenant's NHS-certified mental health crisis treatment lasts plus 30 days, and can easily run for many months.

The 12-month deadline for issuing proceedings is automatically extended for the length of the breathing space.

If rent arrears are "breathing-space debt", the landlord must freeze interest, charges and late-payment penalties on those arrears, stop all enforcement connected with the debt (including instructing bailiffs) and must not contact the tenant. The landlord must also tell any court already handling the claim that the debt is now in breathing space.

Issuing proceedings for an order for possession

Assuming the tenant isn't in a Breathing Space, the landlord can start proceedings using Form N5 (the claim form) and Form N119 (particulars of claim).

The landlord should attach proof of service, a copy of the tenancy agreement and evidence for each ground. For instance, the rent schedule (up-to-date running arrears statement covering two years or from first default), anti-social behaviour diary, photos and witness statements.

The landlord should pay the fee and post the forms and attachments to the local County Court.

If the grounds are exclusively for rent arrears (Grounds 8, 10 or 11), the landlord can do it online with the Possession Claims Online (PCOL) process.[7]

The court will then issue the claim, which means it stamps a sealed copy, allocates a claim number and fixes a hearing date, and sends it to the tenant by first class post. It will also send the landlord a notice of issue confirming the hearing date and the last date for the tenant's defence.

The tenant usually has 14 days to respond to the claim with a defence.

The possession hearing

The next stage is the court hearing, when a judge will decide whether or not to grant a possession order.

At least 14 days before the hearing, the landlord (or their solicitor) should provide a comprehensive, indexed paginated PDF bundle to the court and the tenant.

The bundle should contain everything the judge may be asked to read, for instance, all pleadings, evidence, rent schedule updated to the hearing date (if relevant) and any correspondence. It's particularly important to include anything that has changed since the claim was issued.

At the possession hearing, the judge will already have reviewed the papers, and the case is usually listed for a brief 10- to 15-minute slot. The parties first wait in the corridor, where last-minute agreements are encouraged. Once called in, the landlord or their solicitor outlines the grounds for possession

7. For more details, see *Possession Claim Online: Recover Property*: https://www.gov.uk/possession-claim-online-recover-property.

and the tenant (or a solicitor) may raise a defence, seek more time or propose terms.

Hearings focus on whether the statutory ground is proved and, for discretionary grounds, whether it is reasonable to make an order. Assuming the case is not adjourned, the judge will give an immediate decision, i.e. granting outright possession, making a suspended order with conditions, adjourning with directions or dismissing the claim. The court should issue a sealed order soon afterwards.

If an outright order is granted and the tenant does not leave by the possession date stated in the order, the landlord cannot go to the property to force the tenant to leave but must apply for a warrant of possession.

Enforcing an order for possession

To enforce a possession order, the landlord first waits until the date for possession has passed; if the tenant has not left, the landlord files Form N325[8] (or the PCOL equivalent) with the court and pays the fee.

The court then issues a warrant of possession and instructs its bailiff, who must give the tenant at least 14 days' written notice of the eviction appointment. On the day, the bailiff attends with the landlord (and usually a locksmith), secures the property and returns vacant possession to the landlord.

If speed is important, the landlord can ask the County Court for permission to transfer enforcement to the High Court and

8. Available at: https://www.gov.uk/government/publications/form-n325-request-for-warrant-for-possession-of-land.

use a High Court Enforcement Officer, but this involves extra applications and higher costs.

Whether a tenant moves out voluntarily or after enforcement of a possession order, there are lots of practicalities that a landlord or their agent needs to handle. That is the subject of the final chapter of Part IV.

CHAPTER 16

PRACTICALITIES AT THE END OF A TENANCY

The end of a tenancy can be stressful for landlords and tenants alike. The tenants are usually anxious to get their deposits back promptly and to get a good reference. The landlord is worried what state the property will be left in, and how long the void will be.

This chapter goes through the practicalities involved in managing a smooth end of tenancy for landlord and tenant alike.

1. Pre-check-out inspection

A pre-check-out inspection up to a month before the tenancy is due to end is an effective way of avoiding misunderstandings about how the tenants should leave the property. The goal is a win-win: they get their deposit back in full and you get your property back in good condition. Ideally, you should arrange the pre-check-out inspection before you give your landlord reference.

Take two hard copies of the original Inventory Report: one for you and one for the tenants. Walk through the entire property with them and point out where the property's condition differs from the report. Talk to them about problem areas they need to sort out before they hand over their keys and make a note on your copy.

Here is a checklist of common problem areas for when you do your pre-check-out visit:

CHECKLIST FOR PRE-CHECK-OUT VISIT

Oven and grill. Include any oven dishes/grill pans that you supplied. Unless it's all spotless, explain they will need to clean it thoroughly.

Fridge/Freezer (if supplied). Remind them they must defrost and clean the fridge/freezer.

General cleanliness. Explain that the property will need to be returned in the same state of cleanliness as it was at the start of the tenancy

Carpets. They may need professionally cleaning or cleaning to a professional standard. Point out any stains or burns on the carpet that weren't there when they arrived.

General condition. Check for holes in the walls and doors.

Cellar and attic/loft. Take photos of what's in there and check it against the inventory. Explain that they will need to be clear and clean.

Light fittings. If they have changed any of the light fittings you provided without your permission, explain that the original ones will need refitting by a qualified electrician, and that they'll need to give you a receipt or fitting certificate to prove they were fitted by a qualified electrician.

Walls. If you have given permission for them to put pictures and other items (e.g. TV or shelves) on the wall, explain they will need to fill the holes and repaint, to a professional standard.

Garden. Gardens are often neglected, particularly in winter. Check it against the photos from the inventory and again make clear what they need to remove or replace. Do stress they need to pick up all faeces from dogs or cats that are in the garden or on the paths.

The aim should be to return their deposit in full, if they return the property in a good state. Follow up your visit in writing, pointing out areas that need attention in order for them to receive their deposit back in full.

2. Check-out inventory

Arrange for a professional check-out inventory to be undertaken the day the tenants move out, or the following working day.

The inventory clerk will record the condition of the property and compare it to the check-in inventory, noting whether the wear and tear is excessive and whether the property is in a similar state of cleanliness as it was at the start of the tenancy.

It should be standard for the inventory clerk to take photos of the meter readings for gas, electricity and water, but it is good to check.

Let the tenants know in advance that there will be a check-out inventory after they leave, and this is likely to encourage them to leave the property in good condition.

A professional inventory is inexpensive and fair to both parties.

It will also be an important piece of evidence if they challenge any deductions you wish to make from the deposit.

3. Tenant check-out

As I self-manage, I visit the property myself to do the check-out and take the keys from the tenants.

Ask the tenant for a forwarding address, as usually the Royal Mail redirection service misses a few things, and you will also need to get in touch with them over the return of the deposit. If they have left any items behind, get their consent to dispose of them and deduct the cost from the deposit, and confirm this by email.

4. Utilities

The landlord is responsible for paying for the utilities after the end of the tenancy.

On the last day of the tenancy, it's important to take a photo of the utility meters (gas, electricity and water), or ensure that the company doing the inventory does this, so it's clear exactly what the meters said when the tenancy ended. This will provide evidence about any consumption of gas, electricity and water by the departing tenant, and head off any arguments. I send a copy of the photos to the tenants and ask them to contact the utility companies with their final reading.

I also contact the utility companies to take on an account and give them the starting readings.

As mentioned in Chapter 10, utility companies often do not charge landlords for water during a short void where the property is empty and there is no, or little, water usage.

Consequently, it's important to let them have the water meter readings (where it is metered) and to say that the property is empty.

Sometimes I have to be very insistent to ensure they don't bill me for the standing charge.

5. Council tax

Contact the council to advise them when the tenancy ended. Landlords can usually do this on the council website. Keep a copy of the proof that the notification was sent.

Apart from room-only HMOs, under section 28 RRA, tenants are liable for council tax for the duration of the tenancy, including until the end of the notice period, where they serve notice to end the tenancy.

Once the tenancy ends, the landlord becomes liable to pay council tax. Although some councils give landlords a grace period, most charge landlords the full council tax during voids, and some even add an empty home premium onto the council tax if the property is empty for an extended period.

6. Handling the return of the deposit

Good landlords are fair and reasonable with the return of the deposit. After all, a deposit is a safety net for the landlord, and not a pot to help refurbish the property after the tenants leave.

The deposit remains the tenants' money throughout the tenancy, and the landlord should only make deductions if the tenants damage the property beyond fair wear and tear, for outstanding rent or the replacement of missing items, or where the property is not in the same state of cleanliness as at the start of the tenancy.

This is why it's important to have comprehensive detailed inventories to show what the condition of the property was at the start and end of the tenancy. If the landlord has made improvements to the property since the tenants moved in, they should have evidence of this; for instance, new windows or new appliances.

Fair wear and tear

The landlord should expect fair wear and tear, which reflects the length of the tenancy, the number and age of occupiers, the quality and expected life span of the fixtures and fittings.

For instance, the lifespan of carpet varies from 2–15 years, depending on the quality and whether it is a high traffic area like a hallway. The lifespan of decoration is 3–5 years and ovens from 9–15 years, depending on the quality.

Claiming for your own time

Many landlords are unaware that they may make a small charge for their time in rectifying issues if tenants move out without properly cleaning the property or if there has been excessive wear and tear. It is possible for landlords to claim back costs from tenants for their time and materials, provided they are reasonable.

MyDeposits have stated that landlords may carry out work themselves to rectify excessive wear and tear or to clean the property provided that it does not cost more than employing a contractor and the cost of any materials are reasonable. They suggest £20 an hour as a reasonable hourly rate.[1]

However, landlords can't claim costs for organising the work or travel costs to get to their property. This is because it's part of a landlord's role, even if the work wouldn't have been needed if the tenant left the property in a satisfactory condition.

Deductions

The landlord will need to ask the tenant for their consent to make any deductions. If the tenants don't agree, the tenants (or the landlord) can refer the matter to the dispute resolution service of the deposit scheme.

As with all claims against the deposit, the landlord needs to provide evidence to show the dispute resolution service that any deductions were reasonable and proportionate. The deductions should reflect the expected life span of the item (as explained above), any deterioration of its condition over the course of the tenancy beyond reasonable wear and tear, and any deterioration in the cleanliness of the property compared to check-in.

The precise mechanics of the dispute resolution services differ between schemes, so it's best to visit the website of your scheme if the tenant does not consent to the deductions.

7. What if tenants leave things behind?

Sometimes when tenants move out, they don't take everything

1. MyDeposits, *Resolution Case Study – Cleaning and Landlord Costs*, https://www.mydeposits.co.uk/content-hub/cleaning-and-landlord-costs.

with them, which puts the landlord in a bit of a tricky situation.

It might seem simple to take the items to the tip, or even to sell them. However, the items still belong to the tenants, and the landlord needs to be very careful about disposing of the items.

The Torts (Interference with Goods) Act 1977

Under the Torts (Interference with Goods) Act 1977, the landlord must keep safe any items that tenants leave behind for a reasonable period of time and to take reasonable steps to trace the tenant before disposing of them.

Professionally drafted tenancy agreements will clarify how long the landlord will store items at the end of the tenancy (e.g. 14 or 21 days), with an exception for "waste or refuse", in which case they do not need to be stored. They will also usually enable the landlord to sell any items, provided the landlord first uses reasonable steps to contact the tenant, and to deduct charges for storage from any proceeds of sale.

The tenant can ask for the proceeds of sale up to six years after you send the notice, so don't spend the proceeds of any sale!

Serving the notice

If the landlord can't get hold of the former tenant informally by text, social media or email, they need to send a formal notice under section 12 of the Torts (Interference with Goods) Act 1977 to the last known address of the former tenant.

The notice must contain descriptions of the items and say that low value items will be disposed of, and anything that is valuable will be sold, if the items are not collected by the date, with the costs of storage, disposal and sale deducted from the proceeds of sale.

Steps to follow

Here is a list of practical steps that landlords can do to protect themselves from claims by tenants about items left behind:

- Take photos / videos of all the items the tenants have left behind.
- Make an effort to trace the former tenants, using social media, email, and telephone, and ask them to come and collect their items.
- Draw up a list of the items and categorise as rubbish, low value items and high value items.
- Dispose of the items that are clearly rubbish, e.g. packaging, old house plants, anything broken, and take photos of the disposal.
- If anything is to be sold, obtain a written quotation for the items, including the costs of sale.
- Where a house clearance service is needed, and the items are not valuable, make sure you get this in writing, and keep a copy of any invoice.
- In case the tenant is away or has changed their email address, hold onto sentimental items such as photo albums left in a box in a loft.
- Store all items other than rubbish items safely for the relevant period.
- If the former tenant says to throw it all away, ask for it in writing or at least record the agreement by email or text, and ask for them to confirm agreement.
- Keep detailed records of everything the landlord does.

8. Finding new tenants

The cycle starts again: finding new tenants.

Don't be in a rush to find new tenants straight away. It's easier to let a property that is in excellent condition, instead of looking tired, and it sets the new tenancy off on the right foot. For that reason, when my tenants go, I don't list it for re-letting until after they've moved out. It's easier to do viewings when the property is untenanted as well.

There will usually have been some wear and tear, and a short void is a small price to pay to make sure the property is back to its former excellent condition in time for new tenants. I use the time to attend to any repairs, ensure the property is properly clean, and touch up the walls with paint if there are any marks.

Looking ahead to finding new tenants is a fitting note to bring us to the end of Part IV. In the final chapter, I look ahead more generally.

LOOKING AHEAD

The Renters' Rights Act 2025 has undoubtedly "overhauled" the private rented sector, as promised in Labour's 2024 election manifesto.

This handbook has not discussed the rights and wrongs of the legislation. Instead, I have deliberately focused on the practicalities, not only to help landlords comply with the law, but to share what I believe to be the approach good landlords should take when they provide homes for people to live in.

Looking forward, success as a landlord in the Renters' Rights Act era means embracing the mindset and practices of a "good landlord". The days of "winging it" are over. With complex rules now governing every stage of a tenancy, landlords must operate professionally, stay organised and focus on providing a high-quality service to tenants.

However, being a good landlord isn't about scraping by with the bare minimum. It's about understanding *why* the rules exist and genuinely trying to do right by your tenants. It's not about hunting for loopholes or looking for ways around things. It means recognising that housing is not just another business transaction, but a people-focused service where treating tenants fairly and respectfully benefits all.

Good landlords tend to attract and keep good tenants, and happy tenants stay longer and take better care of the property.

This in turn protects your investment, creating a virtuous circle where both you and your tenants thrive. It not only makes the experience of being a landlord far more rewarding and less stressful, but it also helps elevate the overall standards and trust in the private rented sector.

In view of the extensive powers of investigation that local authorities now have, coupled with the civil penalties they can impose for the breach of most of the duties in the Renters' Rights Act, looking for loopholes is a risky strategy. Litigation is expensive and stressful at the best of times, which is why I tend to err on the side of caution. I don't want to be a test case.

The RRA represents a fundamental shift, raising the bar for what is expected of landlords. If you've read this far, you now have a good understanding of the new regime and what you need to do to comply.

Yes, there are many new rules, from the way tenancies are structured to new registration and documentation duties and stronger enforcement against breaches. However, by adopting the right approach, you can not only comply with the new rules, but you can differentiate yourself as not just a good landlord, but a truly exemplary landlord.

Looking ahead, the rental landscape will continue to evolve. Further changes are already on the horizon with higher energy efficiency standards and Making Tax Digital for unincorporated landlords. It's also likely there will be further revisions to the RRA – it was the same with the Housing Act 1988. Judges will interpret what the RRA means.

Change is the norm in the private rented sector, and the key is to stay informed and adaptable. You can keep up to date with the changes by signing up for my free weekly newsletter here: **theindependentlandlord.com/subscribe.**

Finally, and most importantly, never lose sight of the ethos of the good landlord. If you follow the guidance outlined in this book, not only should you avoid the traps for the unwary, but you're more likely to build positive relationships with your tenants. You'll also be contributing to a better reputation for all landlords and a better private rented sector.

Being a good landlord is good for tenants and good for business.

Suzanne Smith

APPENDIX 1: FURTHER RESOURCES

This appendix pulls together links to useful resources for landlords in one place.

Further support

For more support, you can join my membership community, The Independent Landlord Hub, where you can take all my courses, ask me questions at regular Q&A livestreams and in the forum, and download templates and checklists.

The coupon code **BOOK10** will give you a £10 discount on your first year's membership. You can sign up for the Hub here:

https://theindependentlandlord.com/join-hub.

Keeping up to date

An easy way to keep up to date with developments in the rapidly changing private rented sector, is to subscribe to my free regular newsletter at:

https://theindependentlandlord.com/subscribe.

Landlord accreditation

These are the three leading landlord accreditation schemes for landlords:

- DASH Landlord Accreditation, https://www.dashservices.org.uk/Accreditation.
- London Landlord Accreditation Scheme, https://www.londonlandlords.org.uk/accreditation.
- NRLA Accreditation, https://www.nrla.org.uk/training-academy/accreditation/cpd-activities/accreditation-overview.

Limited companies

There are links to lots of excellent free resources about how to set up and run limited companies on this web page:

https://www.gov.uk/limited-company-formation.

Making Tax Digital (MTD)

The latest from HMRC on MTD for income tax for landlords who own properties in their own name:

https://www.gov.uk/government/collections/making-tax-digital-for-income-tax.

Renters' Rights Act free resources from The Independent Landlord

My free content on the Renters' Rights Act is available here:

https://theindependentlandlord.com/renters-rights-hub.

Renters' Rights Act GOV.UK guidance for landlords

This is the landing page for all the official guidance for landlords and letting agents on renting out property in compliance with the Renters' Rights Act 2025:

https://www.gov.uk/guidance/renting-out-your-property-guidance-for-landlords-and-letting-agents.

Right to Rent guidance

The Government resources on the ever-changing Right to Rent rules are on this page:

https://www.gov.uk/government/publications/landlords-guide-to-right-to-rent-checks.

Statutory forms

You can find all of the statutory forms for free on this Government web page, including Form 3A (the notice seeking possession under section 8 of the Housing Act 1988) and Form 4A (rent increase notice):

https://www.gov.uk/guidance/assured-tenancy-forms.

Taxation

Capital gains tax

Current rates of CGT:

https://www.gov.uk/capital-gains-tax/rates.

What tax is payable when you sell a property:

https://www.gov.uk/tax-sell-property.

Corporation tax

General HMRC guide to corporation tax:

https://www.gov.uk/corporation-tax.

Corporation tax payable when you sell business assets:

https://www.gov.uk/tax-when-your-company-sells-assets.

Income tax

Comprehensive guide from HMRC about income tax payable by unincorporated landlords who own property in their own name: https://www.gov.uk/guidance/income-tax-when-you-rent-out-a-property-working-out-your-rental-income.

Templates and documentation

It is beyond the scope of this handbook to provide template agreements, forms and letters.

However, I provide these in my community, The Independent Landlord Hub:

https://theindependentlandlord.com/join-hub.

The **coupon code BOOK10** will give you a £10 discount on your first year's membership of The Independent Landlord Hub.

Templates and documentation are also available for members of the following organisations:

- Guild of Residential Landlords: https://england.landlordsguild.com.
- Landlord Law: https://landlordlaw.co.uk/join-landlord-law.
- NRLA: https://www.nrla.org.uk/join.

APPENDIX 2: LEGISLATION

Here are links to the various Acts of Parliament, regulations and orders that I mention in the book, arranged in alphabetical order.

Primary legislation

Primary legislation refers to statutes or Acts of Parliament that have been approved by both the House of Commons and the House of Lords and have obtained Royal Assent. It can only be changed through another Act or expressly authorised parliamentary procedure.

Energy Act 2011: https://www.legislation.gov.uk/ukpga/2011/16/contents.

Enterprise and Regulatory Reform Act 2013: https://www.legislation.gov.uk/ukpga/2013/24/contents.

Environmental Protection Act 1990: https://www.legislation.gov.uk/ukpga/1990/43/contents.

Homes (Fitness for Human Habitation) Act 2018: https://www.legislation.gov.uk/ukpga/2018/34.

Housing Act 1988: https://www.legislation.gov.uk/ukpga/1988/50/contents.

Housing Act 1996: https://www.legislation.gov.uk/ukpga/1996/52/contents.

Housing Act 2004: https://www.legislation.gov.uk/ukpga/2004/34/contents.

Housing and Planning Act 2016: https://www.legislation.gov.uk/ukpga/2016/22/contents.

Landlord and Tenant Act 1985: https://www.legislation.gov.uk/ukpga/1985/70/contents.

Leasehold Reform (Ground Rent) Act 2022: https://www.legislation.gov.uk/ukpga/2022/1/contents.

Protection from Eviction Act 1977: https://www.legislation.gov.uk/ukpga/1977/43.

Public Order Act 1986: https://www.legislation.gov.uk/ukpga/1986/64.

Renters' Rights Act 2025: https://www.legislation.gov.uk/ukpga/2025/26.

Social Housing (Regulation) Act 2023: https://www.legislation.gov.uk/ukpga/2023/36.

Tenant Fees Act 2019: https://www.legislation.gov.uk/ukpga/2019/4/contents.

Torts (Interference with Goods) Act 1977: https://www.legislation.gov.uk/ukpga/1977/32.

Secondary legislation

Secondary legislation is law created by ministers under powers given to them by an Act of Parliament. It is often in the form of statutory instruments and referred to as "regulations" or "orders".

The Assured Tenancies (Private Rented Sector) (Written Statement of Terms etc and Information Sheet) (England) Regulations 2026:https://www.legislation.gov.uk/uksi/2026/324/contents/made.

The Electrical Safety Standards in the Private Rented Sector (England) Regulations 2020: https://www.legislation.gov.uk/uksi/2020/312/contents.

The Furniture and Furnishings (Fire) (Safety) Regulations 1988: https://www.legislation.gov.uk/uksi/1988/1324/contents.

The Furniture and Furnishings (Fire) (Safety) (Amendment) Regulations 2025: https://www.legislation.gov.uk/uksi/2025/531/made.

The Housing (Tenancy Deposits) (Prescribed Information) Order 2007: https://www.legislation.gov.uk/uksi/2007/797/contents.

The Licensing and Management of Houses in Multiple Occupation (Additional Provisions) (England) Regulations 2007: https://www.legislation.gov.uk/uksi/2007/1903/contents/made.

The Licensing of Houses in Multiple Occupation (Prescribed Description) (England) Order 2018: https://www.legislation.gov.uk/uksi/2018/221/made.

The Management of Houses in Multiple Occupation (England) Regulations 2006: https://www.legislation.gov.uk/uksi/2006/372/contents.

The Regulatory Reform (Fire Safety) Order 2005: https://www.legislation.gov.uk/uksi/2005/1541/contents.

APPENDIX 3: CIVIL PENALTIES IN THE RENTERS' RIGHTS ACT 2025

Here is an overview of the various civil penalties that the Renters' Rights Act introduces or amends.

1. "Anti-gaming" duties

The "anti-gaming" duties in section 13 of the Renters' Rights Act are designed to prevent landlords and letting agents from circumventing the key tenancy reforms, namely that all assured periodic tenancies are periodic, and they can only be terminated by the landlord in accordance with a valid notice under section 8 of the Housing Act 1988.

Local authorities can impose a civil penalty of up to £7,000 for the first of the following actions:

- Attempting to let for a fixed term in breach of the new s.4A HA88.
- Attempting to end a tenancy by serving a notice that attempts to end a tenancy, in breach of s.5(1) HA88.
- Attempting to end a tenancy, or requiring a tenant to leave, orally, in breach of s.16E(1)(c) HA88.
- Serving an eviction notice on a tenant that attempts to end a tenancy outside the prescribed section 8 process, in breach of s.16E(1)(d) HA88.

- Relying on a section 8 possession ground where the person serving the notice does not reasonably believe the landlord is, will or may be able to obtain an order for possession on that ground, in breach of s.16E(1)(e) HA88, and the tenant the surrenders the tenancy within four months without a possession order.
- Relying on Grounds 1B, 2ZA to 2ZD, 4, 5 to 5H, 6A or 18 without having given the tenant a written statement of terms detailing these grounds at the start of the tenancy, in breach of s.16E(1)(f) HA88
- Re-letting a property before expiry of the 12 month no-let period after using Ground 1 (moving in) or Ground 1A (selling up), in breach of s.16E(2) HA88.
- Marketing a property for let or a licence to occupy or authorising someone to do so before expiry of the 12 month restricted period after using Ground 1 (moving in) or Ground 1A (selling up), in breach of s.6E(3) HA88.

Rental discrimination, rental bidding and pre-tenancy rent payments

The following actions relating to rental discrimination, rental bidding and prohibited pre-tenancy rent payments, are enforceable by civil penalties of up to £7,000:

- Preventing a person from viewing or renting a property on the basis that a child would live with or visit them.
- Preventing a person from viewing or renting a property on the basis that they are a benefits claimant.

- Marketing a property without stating a specific proposed rent figure in the written advertisement or offer.
- Inviting or encouraging a prospective tenant to offer more than the stated advertised rent.
- Accepting an offer from a prospective tenant that is higher than the stated advertised rent.

2. Duty to provide written statements

The Renters' Rights Act contains obligations on relevant persons (landlords and letting agents) to provide certain written statements and prescribed information to tenants.

Local authorities can impose civil penalties of up to £7,000 if landlords do any of the following:

- Fail to provide a tenant with a written statement of the terms of the tenancy before the tenancy is entered into
- Fail to provide an existing tenant with the prescribed information in writing about the changes on the new tenancy system by 31 May 2026 (Information Sheet) [1]
- Relying on certain grounds (i.e. Grounds 1B, 2ZA to 2ZD, 4, 5 to 5H, 6A or 18) without having given the tenant a written statement of terms detailing these grounds at the start of the tenancy

1. *The Renters' Rights Act Information Sheet 2026*, https://www.gov.uk/government/publications/the-renters-rights-act-information-sheet-2026.

PRS Database and PRS Landlord Ombudsman

Landlords may receive a civil penalty of up to £7,000 if they commit any of the following in relation the PRS Landlord Ombudsman and the PRS Database, once launched:

- Failing to join the Ombudsman (or comply with the regulations establishing the Ombudsman), once launched.
- Marketing a property for a residential tenancy without having an active landlord entry and an active dwelling entry in the PRS Database, once launched.
- Advertising a property for let without including the unique identifiers for the landlord and the dwelling in the advertisement or listing in breach of s.82(2) RRA.
- Failing to have active entries for the property and landlord.

The following are offences, for which the civil penalty is up to £40,000:

- Knowingly or recklessly providing information to the Database which is false or misleading in a material respect.
- Continuing to breach Database obligations above (e.g., failing to have entry) after a penalty has been imposed.
- Committing a repeat breach of the Database and Ombudsman duties within five years of the first civil penalty.

Civil penalties for offences

The Renters' Rights Act introduces new offences in the Act itself, and also by amending the Housing Act 1988, Tenant Fees Act 2019 (TFA) and Protection from Eviction Act 1977.

The local council may impose a civil penalty of up to £40,000 as an alternative to prosecution for each of these offences (other than the offence under the TFA which has a maximum civil penalty of £30,000).

- Knowingly or recklessly provides information to the database operator which is false or misleading in a material respect.
- Continuing to breach Database requirements (e.g., failing to register) after a penalty has been imposed, or committing a repeat breach within five years.
- Continuing a breach after a civil penalty has been imposed or repeating a breach within five years.
- Relying on a section 8 possession ground where the person serving the notice knows the landlord would not be able to obtain an order for possession on that ground, or is reckless as to whether the landlord would be able to do so, and the tenant the surrenders the tenancy within four months without a possession order.
- Asking for or accepting rent before the tenancy agreement is signed will be a "prohibited payment" under the Tenant Fees Act 2019. (Up to £5,000 for first breach as this is under the TFA.)
- Unlawful eviction or harassment of a tenant under the Protection from Eviction Act 1977.

APPENDIX 4: IMPLEMENTATION

The Renters' Rights Act (RRA) is being implemented in phases, which is usual for a large and complex new legislation.

Here is a brief overview of the way in which the different provisions of the RRA are due to come into force.

Phase 1: Miscellaneous provisions

As set out in section 145 RRA, the first implementation phase of the Renters' Rights Act was on 27 December 2025, which was two months after the Act received Royal Assent.

The following provisions in the Renters' Rights Act came into force on 27 December:

- Explicit exclusion of long leases from the definition of assured tenancies in the Housing Act 1988, which means that they cannot be evicted under section 8 HA88 regime for non-payment of ground rent.
- New investigatory powers for councils under Chapter 3 of Part 4 RRA.
- Duty for local authorities to report to the Secretary of State on the exercise of their functions under landlord legislation.

Phase 2: Implementation of tenancy reforms

The new assured periodic tenancy regime and associated reforms came into force on 1 May 2026.

This is when all assured shorthold tenancies became assured periodic tenancies, with fixed terms automatically becoming periodic, and the tenancies subject to the new rules regarding written statements, rent increases, rental discrimination, rental bidding, the abolition of "no fault evictions" and the introduction of many new duties and offences, which local authorities can now enforce.

Landlords were required to serve tenants with the official Information Sheet published by 31 May 2026.[1]

Clauses in ASTs entered into before 1 May 2026 requiring rent to be paid in advance remain enforceable.

Section 13 HA88 notices served before 1 May 2026 are valid, but rent increases made under a rent review clause which come into effect after 1 May are not.

Pending notices under section 8 and 21 HA88 continued to be valid, but landlords had until 31 July 2026 to ask the court to issue claim forms for an order for possession.

If a valid section 21 notice was served before 1 May 2026, the tenancy will have continued as an assured shorthold tenancy until either the notice lapsed or the possession proceedings were concluded.

---

1. *The Renters' Rights Act Information Sheet 2026*, https://www.gov.uk/government/publications/the-renters-rights-act-information-sheet-2026.

Phase 3: PRS Database and PRS Landlord Ombudsman

According to the *Implementation Roadmap*, the PRS Database is due to start rolling out regionally in “late 2026”, with the full launch in 2027.

The PRS Landlord Ombudsman is due to be launched in 2028.

Phase 4: Awaab's Law and Decent Homes Standard.

The Decent Homes Standard will come into force for the private rented sector in 2035.

The Government is due to consult on the implementation of Awaab’s Law, and will confirm the date it will come into force after the consultation.

BIBLIOGRAPHY

Association of British Insurers, *Calculating your Rebuild Cost*, https://www.abi.org.uk/products-and-issues/choosing-the-right-insurance/home-insurance/buildings-insurance/calculating-your-rebuild-cost.

British Blind and Shutter Association, *Advice for Landlords on Window Blind Safety* (2021), https://www.makeitsafe.org.uk/wp-content/uploads/2021/04/BBSA-Guidance-for-Landlords-v1-April-21.pdf.

Courts and Tribunals Judiciary, *Awaab Ishak – Prevention of Future Deaths* (16 September 2022), https://www.judiciary.uk/prevention-of-future-death-reports/awaab-ishak-prevention-of-future-deaths-report/.

Department for Communities and Local Government, *A Decent Home: Definition and Guidance for Implementation* (June 2006), https://assets.publishing.service.gov.uk/government/uploads/system/uploads/attachment_data/file/7812/138355.pdf.

Department for Energy Security and Net Zero, *Home Energy Model: Energy Performance Certificates.* Consultation (2026), https://www.gov.uk/government/consultations/home-energy-model-energy-performance-certificates.

Department for Energy Security and Net Zero, *Improving the Energy Performance of Privately Rented Homes in England and Wales.* Consultation (2025), https://www.gov.uk/government/consultations/improving-the-energy-performance-of-privately-rented-homes-2025-update.

Department for Energy Security and Net Zero, *Reforms to the Energy Performance of Buildings Regime* (2024), https://www.gov.uk/government/consultations/reforms-to-the-energy-performance-of-buildings-regime.

Department for Energy Security and Net Zero, *Warm Homes Plan.* Policy Paper (2026), https://www.gov.uk/government/publications/warm-homes-plan.

Department for Environment, Food and Rural Affairs, *Simpler Recycling: Household Recycling in England.* Guidance (2025), https://www.gov.uk/guidance/simpler-recycling-household-recycling-in-england.

Goodlord, *2025 State of the Lettings Industry Report*, https://www.goodlord.com/state-of-the-lettings-industry-report-2025.

GOV.UK, *Check if Someone Can Rent Your Residential Property*, https://www.gov.uk/landlord-immigration-check.

GOV.UK, *Checking Your Tenant's Right to Rent,* https://www.gov.uk/check-tenant-right-to-rent-documents.

GOV.UK, *Make a Court Claim for Money*, https://www.gov.uk/make-court-claim-for-money.

GOV.UK, *Pay the Data Protection Fee*, https://www.gov.uk/data-protection-register-notify-ico-personal-data.

Greater Manchester Good Landlord Charter, https://www.gmgoodlandlord.org.uk.

Health and Safety Executive, *Legionella and Landlords' Responsibilities*, https://www.hse.gov.uk/legionnaires/legionella-landlords-responsibilities.htm.

House of Commons, *"Renters' Rights Bill", Hansard*, 9 October 2024, vol. 754, col. 332, https://hansard.parliament.uk/commons/2024-10-09/debates/7A308DDD-EC0A-4F2D-9C18-664E12D5BC92/Renters%E2%80%99RightsBill.

"Housing 2023: Andy Burnham's keynote speech in full", *Housing Digital* (27 June 2023), https://housingdigital.co.uk/housing-2023-andy-burnhams-keynote-speech-in-full.

HM Revenue & Customs, *Making Tax Digital for Income Tax*, https://www.gov.uk/government/collections/making-tax-digital-for-income-tax.

HM Revenue & Customs, *Property rental income statistics: 2024, Table 13*, https://www.gov.uk/government/statistics/property-rental-income-statistics.

HM Revenue & Customs, *Research Report no.804: Landlords Research Findings* (10 May 2025), https://www.gov.uk/government/publications/landlords-research.

Information Commissioner's Office, *Advice for Small and Medium Organisations*, https://ico.org.uk/for-organisations/advice-for-small-organisations.

Insolvency Service, *Debt Respite Scheme (Breathing Space) Guidance for Creditors*, https://www.gov.uk/government/publications/debt-respite-scheme-breathing-space-guidance-for-creditors.

LACoRS, *Housing - Fire Safety: Guidance on Fire Safety Provisions for Certain Types of Existing Housing* (2008), https://www.cieh.org/media/1244/guidance-on-fire-safety-provisions-for-certain-types-of-existing-housing.pdf.

Maslow, A. H. (1943), "A theory of human motivation", *Psychological Review*, 50(4), 370–396, https://psychclassics.yorku.ca/Maslow/motivation.htm.

Ministry of Housing, Communities and Local Government, *Awaab's Law: Guidance for Social Landlords* (9 January 2024), https://www.gov.uk/government/publications/awaabs-law-guidance-for-social-landlords.

Ministry of Housing, Communities and Local Government, *Building Safety Act 2022*. Guidance (2022), https://www.gov.uk/guidance/the-building-safety-act.

Ministry of Housing, Communities and Local Government, *Consultation on a Reformed Decent Homes Standard* (September 2025), https://www.gov.uk/government/consultations/consultation-on-a-reformed-decent-homes-standard-for-social-and-privately-rented-homes.

Ministry of Housing, Communities and Local Government, *Civil Penalties Under the Renters' Rights Act 2025 and Other Housing Legislation*. Statutory guidance, https://www.gov.uk/government/publications/civil-penalties-under-the-renters-rights-act-2025-and-other-housing-legislation.

Ministry of Housing, Communities and Local Government, Draft Commonhold and Leasehold Reform Bill. Policy paper (2026), https://www.gov.uk/government/publications/draft-commonhold-and-leasehold-reform-bill.

Ministry of Housing, Communities and Local Government, English Private Landlord Survey 2024: Main Report, https://www.gov.uk/government/statistics/english-private-landlord-survey-2024-main-report/english-private-landlord-survey-2024-main-report.

Ministry of Housing, Communities and Local Government, *Guide to the Renters' Rights Act* (2025), https://www.gov.uk/government/publications/guide-to-the-renters-rights-act/guide-to-the-renters-rights-act.

Ministry of Housing, Communities and Local Government, *Historic Renters' Rights Act Becomes Law* (27 October 2025), https://www.gov.uk/government/news/historic-renters-rights-act-becomes-law.

Ministry of Housing, Communities and Local Government, *Home Buying and Selling Reform Consultation* (2025), https://www.gov.uk/government/consultations/home-buying-and-selling-reform.

Ministry of Housing, Communities and Local Government et al, *Housing Health and Safety Rating System (HHSRS) Guidance*. Collection, https://www.gov.uk/government/collections/housing-health-and-safety-rating-system-hhsrs-guidance.

Ministry of Housing, Communities and Local Government, *Implementing the Renters' Rights Act 2025: Our Roadmap for Reforming the Private Rented Sector*. Policy paper (November 2025), https://www.gov.uk/government/publications/renters-rights-act-2025-implementation-roadmap.

Ministry of Housing, Communities and Local Government, *Rent Repayment Orders: Guidance for Local Authorities*, https://www.gov.uk/government/publications/rent-repayment-orders-guidance-for-local-authorities.

Ministry of Housing, Communities and Local Government, *Renting Out Your Property: Guidance for Landlords and Letting Agents – If Your Tenant Wants to Leave*, https://www.gov.uk/guidance/renting-out-your-property-guidance-for-landlords-and-letting-agents.

Ministry of Housing, Communities and Local Government, *Regulation of Property Agents: Working Group Report* (July 2019), https://www.gov.uk/government/publications/regulation-of-property-agents-working-group-report.

Ministry of Housing, Communities and Local Government, *Selective Licensing in the Private Rented Sector: A Guide for Local Authorities*, https://www.gov.uk/government/publications/selective-licensing-in-the-private-rented-sector-a-guide-for-local-authorities/selective-licensing-in-the-private-rented-sector-a-guide-for-local-authorities.

Ministry of Housing, Communities and Local Government, *Tenant Fees Act 2019: Guidance* (2020), https://www.gov.uk/government/publications/tenant-fees-act-2019-guidance.

Ministry of Housing, Communities and Local Government, *Tenant Fees Act amended by the Renters' Rights Act 2025* (2025), Statutory Guidance, https://www.gov.uk/government/publications/tenant-fees-act-amended-by-the-renters-rights-act-2025.

Ministry of Housing, Communities and Local Government, *The New Decent Homes Standard: Policy Statement* (January 2026), https://www.gov.uk/government/consultations/consultation-on-a-reformed-decent-homes-standard-for-social-and-privately-rented-homes/outcome/the-new-decent-homes-standard-policy-statement.

Ministry of Housing, Communities and Local Government, *The Renters' Rights Bill, MHCLG in the Media* (17 September 2024), https://mhclgmedia.blog.gov.uk/2024/09/17/the-renters-rights-bill.

Ministry of Housing, Communities and Local Government, *Understanding and Addressing the Health Risks of Damp and Mould in the Home* (15 August 2024), https://www.gov.uk/government/publications/damp-and-mould-understanding-and-addressing-the-health-risks-for-rented-housing-providers.

MyDeposits, *Resolution Case Study – Cleaning and Landlord Costs*, https://www.mydeposits.co.uk/content-hub/cleaning-and-landlord-costs.

National Residential Landlord Association, S*till Winning – Why Tenants Love Independent Landlords* (24 January 2024), https://www.nrla.org.uk/research/deep-insight/tenant-survey-autumn24?.

Office for National Statistics, I*ndex of Private Housing Rental Prices, UK: January 2022*, https://www.ons.gov.uk/economy/inflationandpriceindices/bulletins/indexofprivatehousingrentalprices/january2022.

OSB Group, *Research: A Future Tenant Standard*, https://landlordleaders.osb.co.uk/collaboration/tenant-research.

*The Housing Act 2004: Licensing of Houses in Multiple Occupation and Selective Licensing of Other Resid*ential Accommodation (England) General Approval 2024 (16 December 2024), https://assets.publishing.service.gov.uk/media/675c57651857548bccbcf9f0/General_Approval_2024.pdf.

Sentencing Council, *Fine Calculator*, https://sentencingcouncil.org.uk/fine-calculator.

ABOUT THE AUTHOR

Suzanne Smith is a portfolio landlord with rental properties, which she manages and lets herself.

Before becoming a landlord, she spent 25 years as an in-house solicitor, 12 years of which were at General Counsel level, most recently as Chief Legal Officer and Company Secretary of Abcam PLC in Cambridge.

She qualified as a solicitor in England and Wales in 1994, and also holds an MBA, a BA in French and an LLB.

After transitioning from the corporate world in 2019, Suzanne built her property portfolio, applying her board-level legal experience to running a successful business as a landlord. When she couldn't find the practical, reliable guidance she needed as a new landlord, she set up The Independent Landlord in August 2022 to fill the gap. A membership community, The Independent Landlord Hub, followed in 2025.

Suzanne's unique blend of legal expertise and hands-on landlord experience has established her as a leading voice in the private rented sector. The Independent Landlord's website, weekly newsletter and YouTube channel now provide tens of thousands of landlords with free, practical guidance every week.

In 2025, The Mortgage Works, the UK's largest buy-to-let mortgage lender, chose Suzanne as their first external content partner, collaborating with her to provide guidance to landlords navigating the changes in the private rented sector.

Suzanne also serves as an independent lay member of Propertymark's disciplinary panel and is a non-executive director of Hello Neighbour Ltd.

With the implementation of the tenancy reforms in the Renters' Rights Act 2025 in May 2026, Suzanne wrote *The Good Landlord Handbook* to provide landlords with a practical manual to help them navigate the new regime, whether they're a first-time landlord using a letting agent or a self-managing landlord with a portfolio of HMOs, and everyone in between.

instagram.com/indie_landlord
linkedin.com/in/suzannesmithlandlord
youtube.com/@indie_landlord

'In my view, having read through the text, this is probably the most comprehensive book on the market today for the private rented sector landlord: there is very little if anything the modern landlord needs to know that's outside the scope of this book. In my view it's a book every landlord (and letting agent) involved in letting property, should read.'
Tom Entwistle – LandlordZONE